BillyBall 2009

The Road to the Phillies-Yankees World Series

Billy Staples and Rich Herschlag

iUniverse, Inc.
New York Bloomington

BillyBall 2009
The Road to the Phillies-Yankees World Series

iUniverse books may be ordered through booksellers or by contacting:

iUniverse
1663 Liberty Drive
Bloomington, IN 47403
www.iuniverse.com
1-800-Authors (1-800-288-4677)

Because of the dynamic nature of the Internet, any Web addresses or links contained in this book may have changed since publication and may no longer be valid.

ISBN: 978-1-4502-5206-5 (sc)
ISBN: 978-1-4502-5205-8 (dj)
ISBN: 978-1-4502-5204-1 (ebk)

Library of Congress Control Number: 2010912586

Printed in the United States of America

iUniverse rev. date: 8/21/2010

Three couples in my life promoted
Love, Loyalty 'n Education
From my heart sincere thanks goes out to
Mom 'n Ron, Kitty 'n Macky and Linny 'n Beall
I thank you, I love you and I respect you

--Billy

To Charles "Pop-Pop" Mann
A better Phillies fan there never has been

--Rich

CONTENTS

FOREWORD BY JIM EISENREICH

About a quarter century ago, I took some time off from baseball to deal with Tourette's. While learning about my illness and plotting my way back to the game, I worked in a friend's archery pro shop. There, in my spare time, I would read articles on the sport of archery, which requires the steadiest of hands, the ability to relax, and total concentration. The best of those articles were written by Dave Staples, founder of the archery Hall of Fame and possibly the sport's greatest advocate. When a column is outstanding, it pulls you away from your immediate surroundings and puts you in a different world—often a better world.

In 2009 I started reading another outstanding column—*Billyball*. *Billyball* wasn't like other baseball columns. This column was about the human side of baseball—the hopes, struggles, and dreams of the people who play the game at its highest level. It's about the childhood experiences that shaped them and who they are today behind the uniform. Sometimes *Billyball* digs deep into the psychology of the game, and sometimes it's hardly about baseball at all.

But *Billyball* is always, one way or another, positive. It's all about human courage and possibilities. Leave the rehashed steroid rumors to someone else. Great things are always happening if you look for them. *Billyball* is the antidote to an era of cynicism, and not just in baseball. Perhaps the biggest miracle of all is that some farsighted publisher actually runs it.

It turns out, however, there are even greater miracles. I learned that Billy Staples, co-writer of *Billyball*, is the son of Dave Staples, Mr.

Archery himself. When I had that conversation with Billy, we realized it was more than just a coincidence. It was an opportunity.

Billy, a former inner city school teacher in Bethlehem, PA, is the founder of Building Education Support Teams (BEST). This organization takes promising, financially challenged high school kids and pays for college in return for a commitment to community service. But it does much more. As the head of a foundation myself, I went with eyes wide open to speak at a recent BEST banquet. There, I watched countless kids—and many graduates of the program as well—walk up to Billy like he was the one person in the world that really cared who they were and where they were going. To them he was "Stapes," and he wasn't simply an educator or a benefactor—he was their mentor

Whether you're hitting a target or a baseball, success in life requires the steadiest of hands, the ability to relax, and total concentration. More importantly, it requires that people with dedication and vision reach out to those around them. The tools may be a bow and arrow. They may be a bat and ball. In this particular case they are a pen, paper, and occasionally a laptop computer.

I'm proud to say that Billy's mission is my mission. If Stapes needs me to visit the projects and talk to a kid who's having trouble, I'm there. If he needs me to see a kid in the hospital, I'm there. I may even agree to write the foreword for *Billyball 2009*.

ACKNOWLEDGEMENTS

So much goodness has occurred since our last book hit the book stores. The success of *Before the Glory* led to an educational speaking tour that has taken me to thirty-nine states and five countries. I have gotten to see a lot of the world because of the success of the book, and I am extremely thankful.

I was able to partner with Carlos Ojeda and Ernesto from SLICK, and their company has sent me to many inspirational speaking gigs. Now I'm SLICK, too! I thank our expert agent, John Willig, for taking on Rich and me as clients. I also want to extend a sincere thanks to Judy Tierney for her expertise on the phone and the computer. She has negotiated every appearance with skill so that I never have to worry about which flight I am on or which hotel I am crashing in. Thanks so much, Judy, for taking care of it all.

In this tough economy I was also able to go house hunting and found a sweet deal in the Nazareth, PA area. I looked at many houses, and my father and I finally spotted the one I bought. It was the last thing we did together before he passed.

As one door closes another opens. Doc Senese and his family made me feel a part of their crew. Doc helped make acquiring a master's degree a reality, and that made my mom a very happy woman.

I can't go without mentioning a few thrills. Broadcasting an inning on television of an Orioles game with legend Gary Thorne was extremely cool, and they practically had to drag me out of there.

Spending time in Minnesota doing pre-game TV with Justin Morneau was a big thrill, and Justin is flat out a class act. Being featured on the *Ed Randall Show* on WFAN radio out of New York City put our book sales over the top! Signing books with Fergie Jenkins and Monte Irvin in Cooperstown during Hall of Fame weekend made Rich and me feel like royalty.

Talking to my idol, Bobby Murcer, one last time before we lost him to cancer is something that will be etched in my mind until I see Bobby and my dad in the next world. Bobby and I spoke at Yogi Berra's golf tournament. When I showed Bobby the dedication to him in *Before the Glory* he was at a loss for words, and tears ran down his cheeks and mine.

Baseball is a visual game, and no matter how colorful the language, a picture definitely is worth a thousand words. A hearty thanks to Yul Heiney, who not only gave us a memorable cover for this project but also helped us tame countless photos en route to the fifty or so that made it in. Yul, you're worth a thousand pictures.

When you visit a ballpark as a journalist, you're in someone's home. Folks like Jim Trdinich of the Pirates and Connie Schwab of the Yankees made us feel like it was our home, too. In and around the Braves clubhouse, Adam Liberman took the open door policy to the next level. And when visiting our home away from home, Citizens Bank Park in Philadelphia, it quickly became apparent that Scott Palmer and Bonnie Clark are in a league of their own.

No door opened wider than the one at *The Trentonian*. Matt Osborne and Aaron Noble are not only top notch editors, they know how to handle extra innings. Bill Murray is tops on the masthead and numero uno in our book. Bill, you had the vision and faith to let us do our own thing. If only you were every teacher and boss we ever had.

Until we meet again, thanks for reading a page or two of either book. We would love to hear from you on Facebook or www.billystaples.com. Three in the morning is fine.

--Billy Staples

Ditto!

--Rich Herschlag

INTRODUCTION:
STEPPING OUTSIDE THE BOX

Sometimes it's hard for guys like us to sit in the press box. There is an unwritten code that you don't cheer, yell, scream, or generally emit any sound above the level of a mild grumble. Should you break the code, even by a decibel, you will find yourself at the center of a dozen or more death stares from the likes of esteemed journalists. So you go back into your shell and wonder where does it all end—with a walk-off grand slam in the seventh game of the World Series and a perfunctory click on MLB.com to see where the pitch was?

When we sat down with publisher Bill Murray and his highly professional staff at *The Trentonian* to discuss the *BillyBall* column, demeanor in the press box wasn't at the top of the list of concerns. Content was. There was already plenty of great baseball reporting from the Harlem River down to Penn's Landing. We wanted to be a little different. We were coming off the great reception of our book, *Before the Glory*, and wondering what the same approach would look like in column form.

It would be filled with offbeat profiles of the players. It would feature stories from their childhood and minor league days and bring insight to who they were. It would take readers into the clubhouse not only to document the mindset of the team before a critical series but during a rain delay when twenty-five professional athletes had to kill an hour watching outtakes from the movie *Anchorman*.

We decided pretty quickly to avoid the usual fare of beaten-to-death controversy—steroid use a dozen years ago, inflated salaries, and off-the-cuff comments blown entirely out of proportion. Instead, we made as conscious a decision as possible to convey the same truths we learned again and again while writing *Before the Glory*—that baseball is chock full of interesting regular dudes and role models, and often they're one in the same.

Turned loose into the wide world of baseball, we had a field day. We watched Manny hold out for a while and later get suspended. Our angle was teammate Juan Pierre's newfound playing time. We watched the media come down hard on A-Rod and interviewed one of his biggest fans—legendary executive director of the Player's Association, Marvin Miller. We watched Dodgers All-Star catcher Russell Martin get second, third, and home stolen off of him by Phillies outfielder Jason Werth and then listened to Martin explain calmly ninety minutes later in a hotel lobby why nothing like that would ever happen again.

It wasn't all light fare. We took in the tremendous loss of Phillies longtime broadcaster Harry Kalas. There was a palpable void at Citizens Bank Park throughout the season. For members of the Phillies family, a remembrance here and there helped fill that void, and a few written words from us made us feel like cousins.

Around late July, there was a subtle change in the atmosphere over the New Jersey Turnpike. The Yankees were beating teams the way they had a dozen years earlier—with seamless defense, timely homeruns, and otherworldy relief pitching. They were even beating the Angels on the road. The Phillies, meanwhile, were finding their '08 legs and were going in for the kill by obtaining American League Cy Young winner Cliff Lee. The table was being set for a possible rematch of the 1950 World Series, but with our luck one of the two teams would get buried in the Divisional Series by a team from somewhere west of the Mississippi.

Our luck changed. As for the Phils and Yanks, it was not a World Series of coincidences or lucky breaks but one of skill and raw talent. With every inning it became more apparent that at the close of the decade the two best teams in the game were ringing it out in style. And with every inning we felt ourselves moving closer to the end of a nearly perfect season, if there is such a thing. We didn't want it to end, and with this volume it doesn't have to.

Baseball is not only a game of inches, but of numbers. In the age of Sabermetrics we had to invent our own statistic for how great '09 was. How many times did we leave the press box to go cheer, yell, and scream in the loge, mezzanine, or a food court? We lost track at the All-Star break.

BRIDGE TO LIDGE ON NIGHT LIKE A FRIDGE

February 9, 2009

A recent Wednesday night in Fogelsville, PA was one of those nights cold enough to throw a monkey wrench into global warming theory. But Mother Nature would have to do a lot better than that to keep about a thousand eager fans away from the local stop of the Phillies Caravan. Outside, it was 3 degrees Fahrenheit with the wind chill factor. Inside, it was 23 days to pitchers and catchers. Outside, with no room left at the Holiday Inn, cars and SUVs were parked on lawns, between dumpsters, and in the Burger King lot, where someone said you might get towed even with a Phillies bumper sticker.

The excitement didn't quite match that witnessed on the National Mall just the day before, during Barack Obama's inauguration, but at times it came close. One thing for sure, the 2009 Phillies have a tougher act to follow than Obama does—the 2008 Phillies.

Inside the conference center, everything from an autographed picture of Joe Paterno to a couple of old seats from Connie Mack Stadium were being auctioned off to benefit local charities like Miracle League of the Lehigh Valley and the Boys and Girls Club of Allentown. Ticket holders lined up to pose for a photo with the 2008 World Series trophy and were cautioned not to actually touch it or hold it over their heads. You might find yourself sitting next to anyone from the guy who fixes your brakes to Cleveland Indians prospect at catcher, Matt McBride. Eight-hundred and sixty-five salads and entrees later, they got down to business.

If you caught the Caravan in York or Williamsport, you might see the likes of a Ryan Howard or a Jimmy Rollins on the dais. At Fogelsville, the current players were Ryan Madson and Scott Eyre. You could say these guys are not household names, but that would really depend on which households you were talking about. The folks who caught a few Phillies games a week during the regular season and every inning of the postseason know these gentlemen comprised roughly half of the "bridge to Lidge." Like the Yankees of the late '90, if the Phillies got to the sixth inning with a lead, you were probably looking at a win.

Eyre was acquired from the Cubs on August 7 and went 3-0 with a 1.88 ERA in 19 games for the Phils. In the postseason he was lights out. Madson, a homegrown Phillie, had a 3.05 ERA in 76 regular season appearances as a set-up man and was very effective in the postseason until the last game of the World Series against the Rays. The entire season was basically crystallized for the Phillies in the suspended final three-and-a-half-inning stint in Game 5. It was bullpen versus bullpen, and the better bullpen won. For Madson, that included an unfortunate homerun surrendered to Rocco Baldelli of the Rays.

Listening to Madson, you can see why the homerun didn't rattle his cage. He smiles and says he spent the 50-hour rain delay hoping he wasn't starting the final three innings. Eyre, meanwhile, explains how much he likes playing for his new team because, as he puts it, "There's not one guy in the clubhouse you can't make fun of." With all the grim, somber pronouncements on cable news every day, it seems the Phillies and their manager, Charlie Manuel, have found an approach to winning that won't burst like a bubble. As a result, the 2010 Phillies might have an even tougher act to follow.

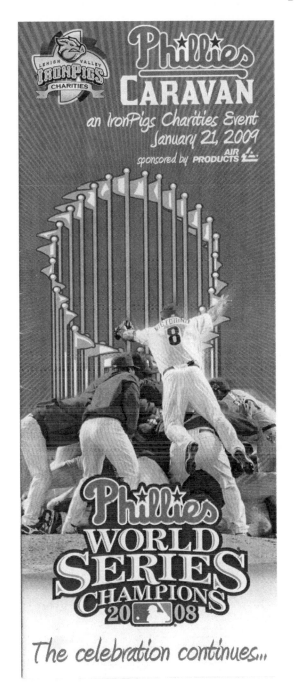

"*It wasn't just a dream.*"

MATTINGLY AND MANNY

February 16, 2009

We caught up recently with former Yankee great and current Dodgers hitting coach Don Mattingly. At forty-seven years of age, he cuts a striking figure. His wrists look like they could still turn on a Roger Clemens fastball inside and remind us that being over forty is no excuse not to be an athlete. In jeans, black t-shirt, and crucifix on a chain, Mattingly is as comfortable in life as he was in the batter's box.

There is, however, a dichotomy in Mattingly's approach to life. The way he puts it, outside the lines he's laid back, West Coast. But between the lines he's all East Coast. That was evident during his years as a player, when he compiled a fielding percentage of .9959—the best ever in the game of baseball—and dominated as a hitter for the better part of a decade until back problems gradually took their toll. As a marquee player in New York, he took advantage of the limelight about as often as he booted a ball, preferring instead to concentrate on the game. Still, he was relaxed and approachable off the field. Beneath the radar, he did an impressive amount of work on behalf of charities.

The split in Mattingly's approach led him to step away from baseball for several years to focus on raising his three sons. The Don Mattingly who returned to baseball in 2004 as the Yankees hitting instructor was somewhere down there on the coaching depth chart as far as experience was concerned. But his knowledge of the game had begun to age like a fine wine. The 2004 Yankees immediately reaped the benefits, hitting a team record 242 homeruns.

After losing out to Joe Girardi in the hunt for the Yankees managerial post following the 2007 season, the up-and-coming coach with the East Coast baseball mentality headed west to join Joe Torre's Dodger staff. Mattingly's impact was just as significant in Chávez Ravine as in the Bronx. On the day after the All-Star break, when Mattingly formally stepped in as hitting coach, the team batting average was .253. The team hit .280 the rest of the way, with team slugging average making a comparable leap. Off course, Mattingly and Torre had help from newly transplanted East Coaster Manny Ramirez, who hit .396 over the final 53 games. But we must remember Donnie Baseball coached Manny down the stretch, too.

During the 2008 season alone, ten Major League managers were relieved of their duties in one way or another. Regardless of how long Joe Torre chooses to stay, 2009, '10, and '11 promise more of the same. Waiting on deck but not dwelling on it is Don Mattingly, with all the street and field cred in the world and a book, *Don Mattingly's Hitting Is Simple*, that is the closest thing this millennium has produced to *The Science of Hitting*, by Ted Williams. In the meantime, Mattingly the maverick has gone to bat for Manny Ramirez, who is in free agent limbo. Mattingly says Manny is all work when standing in at the plate, and who would know better than his hitting coach? Seems like the Yankees, among other teams, should be paying very close attention.

"Donnie Baseball and Billy Baseball."

A-ROD'S A-PPRECIATION

February 23, 2009

These days, only Octo-Mom gets more criticism than A-Rod. A-Rod, however, doesn't deserve all of it. That is not to say he hasn't been part of the culture that has put a massive asterisk on an era's worth of Major League Baseball. His is a celebrity so outsized his confessions make President Obama's press conferences. Heck, these days Alex Rodriguez *is* the asterisk. It doesn't help either when you come back for a second and third at-bat to bury your frank confessions with newly fabricated half-truths and stories so full of holes you could feed them to Nancy Grace for lunch. But the fact remains, A-Rod is not a bad guy.

Not long ago we were talking to Marvin Miller, the legendary executive director of the Major League Baseball Player's Association from the mid-1960s through early '80s. Miller, still an avid tennis player at the age of 91, built the union from a file cabinet in the back of a storage closet to a juggernaut that not only revolutionized Baseball but became the model for all other professional sports.

Miller cut his chops as chief economist for the United Steelworkers of America in the 1950s and '60s. During that time he was invited by three sitting U.S. Presidents to negotiate the country out of a potential labor crisis. So when Marvin Miller arrived on the scene, Baseball owners sensed it was the beginning of the end for $6,000-a-year salaries and maybe even the invincible reserve clause. They just didn't know that they would profit from the change even more than the players.

During the All-Star break in Pittsburgh in 2006, the Players Association held a dinner in Marvin Miller's honor. Players here and there shook his hand. You couldn't blame many of them for saying a few polite words and walking on. Most of them weren't even in diapers when Miller and union attorney Dick Moss won free agency for Andy Messersmith through arbitration. But one player had something he had wanted to say for a long time.

Alex Rodriguez brought his wife with him to greet Marvin Miller and said, "Cynthia, without this man, we wouldn't live the life we live. Our car, house, and everything in it is a direct result of the work this man did many years ago. So we just want to say, 'Thank you, Mr. Miller.'" Miller tried to play it down by saying he was just doing his job and was part of a team. A-Rod knew better. The most celebrated athlete in the game today, the living asterisk, knew Marvin Miller was the brains behind it all, and sometimes even out in front.

That's food for thought the next time a hundred and fifty reporters surround A-Rod and four major cable news networks devote sixty percent of their prime time broadcasts to the identity of Rodriguez's now well-known cousin and his sometimes trainer. Alex Rodriguez has some problems. But he knows history. He is grateful. And he's not afraid to express it.

"Zoned in."

SIGN, MANNY, SIGN

March 2, 2009

Hidden costs are a big topic of discussion these days, whether it's the hidden cost of the Iraq War, the stimulus package, or the deal on your cell phone. Baseball has hidden costs, too. Take the Dodgers, for example. The Los Angeles NL franchise has been holding out a ridiculous sum for Manny Ramirez for more weeks than Obama has collected his executive salary.

In return, Manny has been holding out himself. At latest glance, the offer was a guaranteed $25 million to play this year, with a $20 million option for Manny and agent Scott Boras to take or leave on the table next year. To make the same dough, Obama would have to serve as President till 2122.

Maybe the biggest hidden cost is Juan Pierre. After signing the fleet-footed outfielder to a five year deal prior to the 2007 season at almost $9 million per annum, the Dodgers have both watched and caused Pierre's non-economic fortunes to dwindle. During the second half of last season, with Ramirez playing every day, Juan Pierre was reduced to a bench warmer and occasional pinch runner.

Pierre took it hard, and you can't blame him. Over a seven year period starting in 2001, he averaged about 200 hits, 100 runs, and 50 stolen bases per season. In the middle of that run, he helped lead the Florida Marlins to the 2003 World Series title. The only big knock on Pierre as a leadoff man is that he needs to draw more walks. Nonetheless, the Dodgers' rent-a-slugger program has rudely interrupted a potential Hall of Fame career.

Full disclosure: We may be biased. Back when Juan Pierre was with the Cubs, we a spent a good amount of time interviewing him. He is truly the guy you want your sister to marry, for the additional reason that you get to hang with him. He's cool, laid-back, and gives out some great free memorabilia. He has the original Pac-Man in his living room.

He's fiercely loyal to his parents, brother, and sister. He passed up the gated community for a regular old house in suburban Florida, though he's got a batting cage and full hoops court in the back. In 2005 he quietly donated his time and money to kids from his home state of Louisiana who were displaced by Katrina.

Having established that Juan Pierre is no fourth outfielder and that he doesn't deserve to be left dangling even a minute longer, we need to point out that there is one other hidden cost associated with Manny Ramirez's holdout. Just a few months ago, Ramirez told us how thrilled he was as a newcomer from the Dominican Republic back in 1987 watching his idol, Reuben Sierra, perform at Yankee Stadium. Manny Ramirez cited that golden moment in the Bronx as his first full, personal identification with America.

But at this particular point in American history, it's a little difficult for those of us bagging a lunch, carpooling, using coupons to buy disposable razors, and watching our so-called retirement account sink like a Chien-Ming Wang fastball to hear one more ESPN report of the ex-Red Sox leftfielder shopping around during spring training for a better mid-eight figure deal. So sign on the dotted line, Manny—any dotted line—and spare us all.

"The Dodgers' brain trust?"

O Canada!

March 9, 2009

For many baseball fans, the World Baseball Classic is like a distant tornado watch. You know it's out there somewhere, but if it doesn't preempt the Yankees-Phillies exhibition game on ESPN2, it doesn't quite make the radar.

That's not the case, however, for the players involved in the tournament and a growing number of baseball fans across the globe. It is especially not the case for Team Canada. This is a squad with something to prove. We felt that special aura the moment we stepped into their clubhouse in Dunedin, Florida just before the team's exhibition game with the Toronto Blue Jays.

Team Canada franchise player Justin Morneau is pumped. He has many reasons to be. The 2006 American League MVP is newly married to his bride, Krista, after writing his proposal in the sand during winter vacation. His summer team, the Minnesota Twins, staged their usual late-season surge in 2008 and forced a one-game playoff with the Chicago White Sox. But foremost in Morneau's mind before taking BP in Dunedin is shocking the world.

Morneau points out that Team Canada has players representing 19 Major League systems. Ten of the players currently occupy a spot on a Major League roster. The core of that group consists of Red Sox All-Star outfielder Jason Bay, Dodgers All-Star catcher Russell Martin, and first baseman Morneau. The folks fleshing out the core are no scrubs. They include former Twins star third baseman Corey Koskie, Twins middle reliever Jesse Crain, and Matt Stairs. Stairs of the Phils, if you recall, shocked Los Angeles with a Game 4 pinch hit two-run homerun in the NL Championship Series.

As for the rest of Team Canada, Morneau warns Teams USA, Dominican, Japan, and Mexico not to get too comfortable. "No one has ever heard of most of the guys on our pitching staff," he says. "And that's to our advantage." Also to Team Canada's advantage is home field during the first round in Toronto, where they play Derek Jeter and Team USA. Last but not least, Canada is managed by former Toronto Blue Jays All-Star catcher Ernie Whitt and coached in the batter's box by British Columbia legend Larry Walker. Not since the first season of *Second City Television* has so much Canadian talent been assembled in one place.

No doubt Morneau and company have sweet visions of becoming world class underdogs piling on in celebration like Mike Eruzione and the USA men's hockey team defeating the Soviet Union, then Finland at Lake Placid in the 1980 Winter Olympics. Whether or not that happens, there is a bigger picture, and it's not merely the extra at-bats Justin Morneau's Minnesota Twins backup, Brian Buscher, gets while Morneau is off this spring conquering the planet.

Just as the USA's utter predominance in steel, cars, and skyscrapers is a thing of the past, so it is in baseball. But here is the silver lining. Any economist worth his tattered copy of Adam Smith's *The Wealth of Nations* will tell you global competition makes everyone stronger. In baseball's age of steroid revelations, overpriced seats, and economic downturn, that can only be a good thing.

"Justin spreads the word."

SPRING FLING

March 16, 2009

To paraphrase Mark Twain, reports of baseball's death are greatly exaggerated. There is nothing quite like the Tampa Bay area in March for overgrown kids looking to OD on America's pastime and turn back the often unkind hands of time.

Our own fantasy camp consisted of six ballparks and eleven teams in eight glorious days. The facilities in Dunedin, Lakeland, Tampa, Clearwater, Fort Meyers, and Bradenton are separated by twenty miles here, thirty miles there and tucked away behind strip malls and VFW halls. But with a GPS navigation system, you can travel half-brain dead and think about more important things, like whether they'll stock the Tigers press box with Mountain Dew.

Coming from a region of the country where the sound of your neighbor trying to start his Honda Accord serves as an alarm clock, you are in for a shock when you spot your first five-day forecast. You see so many 80s you're not sure if you're looking at your wife's diastolic blood pressure readings or your kid's report card. Inside the tidy, modest stadiums, the grass is so perfectly matted you reach down once or twice to make sure it's real.

Most striking of all is how genuinely happy people are. The recession looms large beyond the camps, with Tampa Bay's unemployment rate edging to 9.7 percent this month. But local people and folks from around the country can still scrape together the ten or twelve dollars to get in to a game. Euphoric fans cram up against the foul line fences to snatch an autograph, whether from a big name like Phillies Manager Charlie Manuel or a long shot non-roster invitee wearing number 90 like Reds catcher Chris Denove. And we would be remiss if we did not mention that of all the cities represented, the Phillies had the hottest contingent of female phanatics from back home.

Kids are all over the place. And not just the really little ones waving their first Pirates pennant and eating their first rubbery ballpark frank. Kids like Phillies hopeful John Mayberry Jr. taking a curveball for a strike in Dunedin while his father, former Royals slugger John Mayberry, bites his nails in the stands.

Kids like Adam and Andy LaRoche who bat back-to-back for the Pirates at McKechnie Field in Bradenton while a half hour away their father, former All-Star reliever Dave LaRoche, tells Blue Jays hurlers to keep the ball low. Or kids like Travis Snider of the Jays, who doesn't have a famous dad but who was the youngest player in Major League Baseball last year and calmly goes two for three against the Reds in Dunedin.

But the kids who surprise you most, it turns out, are not even at the ballpark. Every day before heading out to one complex or another, we stopped in for a Kiwi Island Treat at the Smoothie King on Dale Mabry Highway in Tampa. The two sharp young ladies behind the counter always mixed in just enough B-12 and knew a lot of players' names. On day five, when they heard we were headed out to Lakeland, where the Tigers train, they told us to say hello to their dad.

We were just about ready to write down the name of an assistant press secretary or the public address announcer when they mentioned their dad was Gary Sheffield, that Tigers designated hitter with one homerun to go to reach five hundred. While their father could probably afford to buy the Smoothie King on Dale Mabry plus another in every small town up the Gulf Coast, he apparently thinks it's a good idea for his kids to get some experience actually working for a living.

It was just that kind of moment—a friendly blur between famous and not-so-famous, between out-of-towner and local—that made our week and a day in baseball land a working vacation that was more vacation than work.

Of course, if all of this was as great as we say, you might ask why did we come back up north? Simple--because we had to.

"Let's win two!"

THE LEGACY OF NUMBER 8

March 23, 2009

The great philosopher John Lennon said life is what happens to you while you're busy making other plans. Our plans at Lakeland, Florida one afternoon in spring training were to hang out by the Yankees clubhouse and see if we could get a few words from Johnny Damon or Nick Swisher about the kind of platoon system they anticipated in 2009. And then another great philosopher, Yogi Berra, rolled toward us in a golf cart. We saw the fork in the road and we took it.

Yogi's first spring training was in 1947, the year Jackie Robinson was the talk of the Grapefruit League. Since then, Berra has been to every spring training in one capacity or another, making it 63 straight. That's a record that will stand until it's broken.

Yogi shared with us some details of his early Florida springs with still another great sage, Yankees manager Casey Stengel. Stengel was not exactly a disciplinarian, but he had rules. As much as he loved kids, they were not allowed in the clubhouse after the game unless the Yankees won. That was enforced even in a split-squad game where Charlie Silvera was the catcher.

Like just about every other big league manager of the era, Casey didn't allow music in the spring training clubhouse, win or lose. No Count, no Ella, no Sinatra, no Elvis, no Hank. Just the rhythm of cleats hitting the concrete floor. Players weren't allowed to drive their car to the game. Everyone had to get on the team bus, even if it was just a ten minute drive up the road from St. Petersburg. The bus ride was sans music too, at least until Phil Linz and his harmonica joined the team in the early '60s.

Suddenly on this perfect day in Lakeland, another fork in the road arrived, and it took its own course. An autograph seeker showed up, but he wasn't four-foot-three with a ketchup stain at the corner of his mouth or three hundred pounds with an eBay account. It was tall, lean Gerald Laird, number 8 of the Detroit Tigers. We didn't really know Laird's deal, but sometimes you can observe a lot just by watching.

Laird grew up a fan of the game in southern California and followed the careers of All-Stars like Dale Murphy and Ivan Rodriguez. Laird himself was drafted by the A's in 1999 and came up in the Texas Rangers organization as a defensive catcher. Sharing duties behind the plate between 2003 and 2008, he threw out an otherworldly forty percent of runners attempting to steal.

Last season, Laird added to his repertoire a respectable batting average of .276. Before the start of this season, he was traded for two minor league pitchers to the Detroit Tigers. According to the Tigers, Gerald Laird is now their number one catcher and heir apparent to his boyhood idol, Pudge Rodriguez.

Laird is a thoughtful guy who told us minutes before game time he was never too busy to stop and connect with greatness and history if he had the chance. He wore a huge smile when Yogi signed for him, and you could still imagine the ketchup stain.

It ain't over till it's over. But then the National Anthem played, and it was indeed over. Laird was off to try to do justice to all the great number 8's before him—Gary Carter, Javy Lopez, and maybe one day even Berra himself. But the consolation was we'd be back next year—Yogi for spring training number 64, Laird with an All-Star type season under his belt, and us with a more compact tape recorder. It will be déjà vu all over again.

"Pair of eights."

THE CONSTANT GARDNER

March 30, 2009

Even though Death Valley at Yankee Stadium has shrunk over the years like cameras, cell phones, and pension plans, it still takes a lot of footsteps to cover centerfield. The hardest footsteps are the ones you're following in. Meusel, DiMaggio, Mantle, Murcer, Henderson, Williams—it's like a dynasty within a dynasty.

Though rumors are still swirling like the wind on a cold day in April at The House That Ruth Built, it's looking more and more like the successor to the throne will be Brett Gardner. At press time, Gardner's spring training batting average was .400 to go along with an on-base percentage of .460 that would make anyone but Barry Bonds on steroids proud. Throw in four stolen bases and three homeruns, and you've got a fast track to center stage on opening day.

The speedy Yankees centerfielder of the immediate future was gracious enough to slow down and talk to us on his way to the clubhouse during an exhibition game against the Pirates at McKechnie Field. No slight against Melky Cabrera, who is also having a good spring, but if there are extra points for being relaxed and accessible, Gardner is a lock.

Gardner grew up in Holly Hill, South Carolina a baseball and country music fan. By 1990, when Gardner was seven, Pete Rose was out of baseball, but the grainy highlight reels made an impression on the fleet-footed Little Leaguer. Gardner noticed the way Rose seemed to give a hundred percent whether legging out an infield hit or looking for a piece of lumber in the bat rack. A light went on in the young player's head, and it never went off.

Watching Ken Griffey Jr. in the 1990s further influenced Gardner, who observed that whenever the television camera happened to show Griffey, he was having fun. Smiling and wearing his cap backwards made Griffey one of the very rare six-tool players. Today, Brett Gardner can hit, run, field, and smile with the best of them. The arm is decent, and as a lefty with bat speed at new Yankee Stadium (the dimensions are still the same), Gardner may one day be a five-and-a-half-tool player.

He was a walk-on at the College of Charleston and led the nation with a .447 batting average in 2005 before the Yankees drafted him in the third round. His .291 lifetime batting average in the minors includes two standout half-seasons for that fabulous Yankees proving ground known as the Trenton Thunder. In 2006 in our backyard, Gardner stole 28 bases and scored 41 runs in a brief 217 at-bats.

Gardner picked up more than baserunning prowess in the Northeast. During his days with the Staten Island Yankees he met his future wife, Jessica, a basketball teammate of Gardner's sister at Wagner College. This past November, Brett and Jessica's garden grew when their son, Hunter, was born. One day, Hunter will be watching highlight films of his dad chasing down fly balls to the 408 mark, but with Blu-ray technology they won't be grainy.

As far as country music goes, there is less than complete harmony in the Gardner home. Jessica prefers Toby Keith, while Brett favors George Strait. Strait isn't the flashiest performer around, but he does have 56 number one hits, and if you're an aspiring Yankees centerfielder, that's an auspicious number.

The record books on the old Yankee Stadium are closed. But if there were indeed ghosts in The House That Ruth Built, you can bet they'll make their way across the street to The House That Jeter Built. We're betting they won't faze Gardner come April and that the new Yankees centerfielder will be more than just the answer to a trivia question one day.

"Ready to grow."

Jon Runyan and Zach Kraus:
Two Heroes, One Goal

April 2, 2009

On the Wednesday before the January 11 playoff game with the New York Giants, veteran Eagles offensive tackle Jon Runyan rearranged a full day of practice and numerous other obligations to go to the hospital. The problem had nothing to do with Runyan's six-foot-eight, three-hundred-and-thirty pound body. Runyan's destination was St. Christopher's Hospital for Children in Philadelphia. There, thirteen-year-old Zach Kraus's life hung in the balance.

Kraus had been battling acute lymphocytic leukemia for the past seven years and was thought to be close to the end. Runyan ducked slightly to get through the door to Kraus's hospital room and told him to hang in there and keep fighting. Runyan spent a good hour with Kraus, and it was the beginning of something special.

Runyan's early exit from practice didn't seem to hurt his performance. It might even have helped. Though it wasn't quarterback Donovan McNabb's best game, one thing apparent to everyone who watched that day was how much time McNabb had on most plays, even against the Giants' fearsome pass rushing game. That kind of time allowed McNabb to make key plays like the 1-yard touchdown pass to Brent Celek in the fourth quarter.

The visit seems to have helped Zach Kraus, too. His mom, Tamara, noticed a difference right away. More than a month or so later, he is not only alive, but walking around and visiting friends. His white blood cell count has improved, and there is new hope medical science can't quite explain. Today, the day after Valentine's Day, we set out to try and explain it ourselves.

At Jon Runyan's home in Mount Laurel, New Jersey, there is a reunion of sorts. Zach Kraus is here with his mom. Jon Runyan is here with his wife, Loretta; their three kids, Jon Daniel Jr., Alyssa, and Isabella; and their pet hog, Lucy. We're here, too, as privileged guests interviewing not one but two superstars.

Ironically, Zach is a little more mobile than Jon today. Zach is in his wheelchair most of the time but has little trouble getting around. Jon has recently undergone arthroscopic microfracture surgery on his right knee, which is immobilized. If you think it's hard getting out of a chair when you can't bend your knee, try it at six-foot-eight. Runyan has about two months to go in this condition. During that time, fibrocartilage, or what can more easily be understood as scar tissue will form, reconnecting bones and doing the job that the original cartilage used to do.

At that point, when the cast comes off, Jon Runyan—who hasn't missed a game in his legendary thirteen-year career as a starting NFL offensive lineman—will begin to learn to walk again. Let alone learn to push defensive ends like Osi Umenyiora back from the line of scrimmage.

Runyan is looking forward to the fight. That's not an attitude he picked up in the National Football League. He brought it there with him. If you ever happen to see a documentary called *Roger and Me*, look for the Runyans or a family like them. Growing up in Flint, Michigan in the 1980s put young Jon Runyan in the heart of the General Motors layoffs and ultimately the plant closing.

Jon's dad, Tom, was a machine repair specialist for GM. Tom was the kind of guy who could take apart anything and put it back together again. He was also an innovator who could redesign machines to perform better. Tom was urged to go back to school and get his engineering degree, but that meant years of studying at night for a twenty thousand dollar a year pay cut.

The decision became moot when Tom Runyan was laid off. The layoff lasted three long years. Tom took odd jobs and even opened a bicycle repair shop, but times were tough for him, his wife Janice, and their three sons. Son Jon recalls the upper floor of their Cape Cod home being sealed off during the cold months to save on heat.

Meanwhile, Jon Runyan, a mechanically inclined kid himself, had a battle of his own. Difficulty reading led to some tests for dyslexia, but when he placed just beyond the range of dyslexic, the result was no tutoring or any other special help. Runyan continued his self-styled approach to reading, which basically entailed a "no-phonics" method. He would memorize the appearance of thousands of words, one word at a time.

The combination of the stress at home and the struggle at school is something Jon Runyan remembers as clearly as memorized words to this day. He would leave the house early to avoid dealing with the friction. At school he was always known as easygoing, but there was now an edge to him. When one mischievous classmate knocked Runyan's books loose all over the hallway, the culprit realized quickly he had bitten off a lot more than he could chew. Unfortunately for him, Jon Runyan had grown to full height by age fifteen.

Today, Jon's dad has comfortably retired and taken up fishing. Jon Runyan has memorized more words than John Madden can spew out on any given Sunday and is a prolific reader—though by his own account boring stuff still puts him right to sleep. But those early struggles reshaped his DNA and now turbo-charge his personal road to recovery.

As the clock on our roundtable discussion winds down, we are first and goal. Of the six kids that were diagnosed all those years ago along with Zach Kraus, he is one of only three still going. He explains that what gets him through spinal taps and chemotherapy are thoughts of getting his full strength back, hanging out with his friends, going to the movies, going to school, and maybe even playing competitive baseball one day. Add to that list watching number 69 put a hurting on defensive tackles. Zach Kraus is a certified Jon Runyan fan now. He sees in his friend "the power and strength to push himself through, to make it to every game no matter what."

Jon Runyan is an even bigger Zach Kraus fan. He explains that he and Kraus share a trait many people don't have, or perhaps don't know they have—the ability to find something out there beyond the immediate circumstances and project themselves there, 24/7 if necessary. For Jon Runyan, his storied career is on the line. For Zach Kraus, his life.

Right now, both heroes are projecting to the second week in September. Jon will be running through a stadium tunnel on a warm Sunday afternoon, starting his 193rd consecutive regular season game. Zach will be there, too, if not in the tunnel then in a seat nearby, whether in Philadelphia or some other NFL city. In this new era of "Yes we can," Zach and Jon have made a pact, and only fools and Monday morning quarterbacks will doubt them.

"Billy in a hero sandwich."

THE LEGEND OF GEORGE KELL

April 6, 2009

An otherwise glorious spring in baseball grew a little dimmer on March 24 with the passing of Hall of Fame Tigers third baseman George Kell. Darker still for those of us who had the pleasure of knowing him. Kell's exploits are legendary. He was selected to ten All-Star teams. He finished in the top ten for the American League MVP award three times.

Kell hit .300 or better seven consecutive seasons and batted .306 for his career. In 1949, he nudged out Ted Williams by two tenths of a point for the American League batting crown. That season he struck out all of 13 times, or what Ryan Howard calls a four-game series. In his final two seasons, playing for the Orioles, Kell became mentor to the next great third baseman, Arkansas compatriot Brooks Robinson.

One chilly fall evening a couple of years ago, during the Philadelphia A's reunion at the Days Inn in Horsham, George Kell, in the same easygoing sonorous voice that made him a beloved Detroit Tigers broadcaster for almost forty years reeled off one obscure entertaining yarn after another. Among the funniest was the story of how he got to Philadelphia the first time.

Kell grew up the oldest son of a barber in the one-horse, no-stoplight town of Swifton, Arkansas. The Brooklyn Dodgers signed him after a year of college for a little more than nothing to their class D team in Newport, Arkansas. As a shortstop and third baseman, Kell had a rough couple of months in 1940, hitting .160. But in 1941, Kell's first full year of pro ball, he was moved to third base permanently, batted .310, and thought he was on his way to the big leagues.

Kell's next stop was the Dodgers' Class B club in Durham, North Carolina. Durham was no bull. About sixty talented players were invited to camp that spring, and seven of them were third basemen. Kell was among two dozen or so players released after hardly getting a chance to field a bad hop. But Kell had another problem. He didn't have the money for the train ride back to Swifton, and his father didn't have it to wire to him.

So, in what can be described as a sort of very early episode of *Seinfeld*, George didn't go home. He kept hanging around the hotel in Durham, eating meals with the roster players, talking baseball, and taking naps upstairs in a room that was no longer his. After about a week, Durham club officials told him, "Hey, you really have to be moving along now!" George explained he was looking for a job in town to save up train fare.

The Durham front office people didn't know what to believe, but they knew they wanted George out of there. So when the Lancaster Red Roses, the Pennsylvania team from the Interstate League, came in to town for a game, the Durham folks talked up George's baseball skills—the same skills they had never really seen. The ploy worked. Lancaster took George off their hands and gave him $300 a month, a better salary than he made during his cup of coffee with the Durham Bulls.

That season with Lancaster, Kell hit .299. The next year he hit .396, and even the Amish took note. The Red Roses, it turned out, were an affiliate of the Philadelphia A's. When at the end of the 1943 season Connie Mack—with suit, tie, and straw hat—stepped into the Lancaster clubhouse and told George Kell he had bought out his contract for $20,000, the third baseman from Swifton thought he had seen God.

W.C. Fields said he spent a year in Philadelphia one Sunday. George Kell spent a little over two years in the City of Brotherly Love and loved every day of it—enough to come back numerous times to the A's reunion and entertain us all. To George Kell, Hall of Famer, we give an opening day salute.

"George and Rich."

MUDCAT, OBAMA, AND HISTORY

April 13, 2009

Recently, we called Jim "Mudcat" Grant to talk baseball. But we didn't talk that much baseball. There was still snow on the ground, the Dow Jones was buried somewhere below, and anybody you spoke to had an opinion on whether Obama could get us out.

Mudcat, however, is not just anybody. He grew up the second youngest of thirteen children in Lacoochee, Florida in the 1930s and '40s. His grandmother and mother knew the vestiges of slavery not to mention Jim Crow firsthand. Among Mudcat's earliest memories were those of his mother putting him down by the fireplace until the Ku Klux Klan was done firing shots into the house.

When Mudcat was five his father died of pneumonia while working for a logging company where there was no such thing as a sick day. Mudcat learned to read using books pieced together from the tattered remains graciously provided by the state education department.

No one guessed that James Timothy Grant would one day become the first African-American to win twenty games in the minors or to win a World Series game in the AL. No one guessed he would win 21 for the Twins in 1965 when he was the Sporting News Pitcher of the Year, rack up 145 wins lifetime, or appear in 80 as a reliever in 1970 while posting an ERA of 1.86.

And no one supposed the kid from Lacoochee would meet President John F. Kennedy and Dr. Martin Luther King Jr. or be mentored as a musician by the likes of Duke Ellington and Count Basie. But the way seventy-three-year-old Mudcat sees it, his greatest single day lies ahead of him.

When Grant first really noticed Barack Obama, the former All-Star and current baseball ambassador was already thinking about Hillary Clinton as the next U.S. President. But in the days leading up to the Iowa Caucus, Grant recognized in Obama an eloquence, well-rounded intelligence, and unquantifiable self-confidence he had observed on the scene only once or twice per generation.

Still, Mudcat didn't expect an Obama presidency any more than he expected to hit a homerun as the winning pitcher in Game 6 of the 1965 World Series. As an African-American, he saw Jesse Jackson's runs in 1984 and 1988 as "a good, hard first knock on the door." Grant figured it would take three such knocks to open the door and assumed Obama's was knock number two.

Like millions of Americans from various backgrounds, Mudcat Grant felt chills when Obama took the oath of office. But like only a very few, Grant vividly imagined a roundtable discussion with preceding pioneers he called his friends—people like Jackie Robinson and like Larry Doby, the power hitter who broke the color line in the Junior Circuit. Mudcat was at one time Robinson's batboy and later his peer. Grant also went from being Doby's number one fan to being his roommate with the Cleveland Indians.

As Grant hears it, Robinson would give Obama a detailed description of the people who didn't want him in there and who desperately wanted him to fail. Robinson would let the President know, however, that whatever he might feel outside the lines, once he crossed those lines it was time to win. Doby would take a more jovial approach, slapping Mudcat on the back and shouting, "Roomie, we made it!"

Both Jackie Robinson and Larry Doby would let the President know he'll be earning more than a few prematurely gray hairs and to wear them proudly. Both would take a moment to pray the President enjoy at least four years in safety and good health. Finally, both would agree with their protégé Mudcat that the best shield of all for Obama, and perhaps his greatest asset, is his lack of any discernable bitterness.

Less fantastical than this celestial meeting of legends is the day when Mudcat Grant gets to meet Barack Obama. On that day, Mudcat tells us, he will have a tremble in his chest and will be surrounded by the spirits of King, Kennedy, Robinson, and Doby. It takes us, however, to point out that President Obama, athlete and Chicago White Sox fan, will have a gleam in his eye, too.

Oh yeah—Mudcat likes Minnesota in the AL Central this year.

"Very valuable players: Mauer and Mudcat."

MAKING THE MAJORS THE LONG WAY

April 20, 2009

There is a glass ceiling separating different stations in life. Perhaps nowhere is that glass thicker than between the minor leagues and the Major Leagues. You can envision breaking through a thousand times, but if you're ever fortunate enough to do it the experience will probably be like nothing like the dream.

As of early July 2008, Mike Cervenak of the Triple-A Phillies had well over twelve hundred hits in the minor leagues. As a sure-fielding first and third baseman, he had hit well over .300 multiple times with farm teams in the Yankees and Giants organizations, was closing in on 150 homeruns, and was a perennial minor league All-Star.

With the Ironpigs of the Lehigh Valley, Cervenak was doing what he had done for about a decade when on July 10 the call finally came. The contending Phils needed an extra bat coming off the bench just before the All-Star break, and Cerv was that bat. His first big league at-bat the very next day was an opportunity at Citizens Bank Park to pinch hit for reliever J.C. Romero against the Diamondbacks.

All sorts of thoughts went through Cervenak's mind in the on-deck circle, from growing up outside Detroit in the early '80s studying Tigers shortstop Alan Trammell's compact swing, to celebrating the Tigers' 1984 World Series victory at his grandmother's house by making confetti out of old lottery tickets, to leading the University of Michigan Wolverines to a Big Ten championship, to a short stint with the Kia Tigers of Korea where simply going out to buy milk and butter was an adventure. But there was no little time to dwell. Ryan Howard was on first base in an extra-inning game. Swinging a bit late at a slider would mean grounding into a double play.

Cervenak made a small statement by flying out to the track in left field. That was still his only at-bat when he was sent back down to Triple-A a few days later. A second call-up came on July 29 when Pedro Feliz was injured. Cerv describes the next few days on the bench as a personal hell for a newly minted Major Leaguer. "You have an eternity to think, and all I could think was, *I just want to get that first damn hit!*"

If you're one of the many minor league fans who've had the pleasure of watching Mike Cervenak hit, you know he's a surgeon at the plate. He has George Brett's efficient swing courtesy of training videos from hitting instructor Charlie Lau. Cerv waits calmly but sees his pitch virtually before it leaves the pitcher's hand and then strikes quickly, viciously, yet calmly.

On August 6 against the Marlins, Cervenak got a long-awaited second chance pinch hitting for Kyle Kendrick and chopped a 3-1 pitch over third baseman Jorge Cantu's head for not only his first Major League hit but also his first RBI, to go with about seven hundred in the minors. According to smiling Mike from Michigan, the weight of the world was off his shoulders. The glass ceiling was shattered into a thousand pieces.

Cervenak would have only a few more at-bats in the show the rest of the season. But any remaining shards of glass along the inside of the frame were stripped away when Cervenak and teammates Andy Tracy, Greg Golson, and Lou Marson were called up to sit on the bench during the playoffs and World Series. They were reserves available for activation the following game in case there was an injury. Cerv was humble while taking batting practice, feeling a little bad for the roster players shagging fly balls in the cold from the bat of a guy not eligible to play that day.

The rest, of course, is history. Cervenak and friends were on the pile amidst ten thousand flashes and forty-five thousand screaming fans seconds after Lidge closed the door on the Rays. What Mike Cervenak couldn't have guessed was that in early April 2009, Phillies President David Montgomery would drive an hour up the Turnpike to Coca-Cola Park to deliver Cervenak, Tracy, Marson, and Kendrick their

World Series rings personally. It was this gracious act by the Phillies organization that, as much as anything else, made Cervenak a Major Leaguer.

"Cerv and Bill."

Jordan Zimmermann Brings Hope to Nation's Capital

April 27, 2009

Anyone who has any money left these days wants in on the ground floor of something big. By interviewing Jordan Zimmermann five days before his first Major League start, we got in on a ground floor of sorts, and it didn't cost a dime.

We admit to having visions, years from now, of telling we-knew-Jordan-Zimmermann-when stories around the poker table. At the same time, we know this thing called big league baseball is a volatile market, especially when it comes to that commodity known as the phenom pitcher.

The history of such super-hyped prospects ranges from seventeen-year-old farm boy Bob Feller striking out 76 batters in 62 innings for the Cleveland Indians in 1936, to Joe Nuxhall getting shellacked for five runs in two-thirds of an inning at the tender age of 15 years and 316 days before achieving success much later, to one solid start for eighteen-year-old Texas Ranger David Clyde in 1973 before experiencing a descent almost as fast as the Dow Jones in '08. There was even another Jordan Zimmerman, with one "n," who, pitching for the Seattle Mariners in 1999, surrendered seven earned runs in eight innings and was never heard from again.

This Jordan Zimmermann—the right-hander from Auburndale, Wisconsin—is a much better bet in the futures market. Like Bob

Feller, he's a farm boy with a blazing fastball. Zimmermann has been clocked in the mid-90s and has a slider growing nastier by the game. But at twenty-two, Zimmermann is not exactly being thrown to the wolves. When he was seventeen his fastball barely reached the mid-80s. Receiving only a half-hearted offer from the University of Minnesota, Zimmermann chose to stay close to home and attend the University of Wisconsin—Stevens Point, a small Division III school.

For Jordan Zimmermann, there was a lot to like about home, even with his parents divorcing when he was only two. Jordan and his mom, Kris, lived at the outskirts of her parents' farm. The two would stay in shape lifting bales of hay, one after the other. Jordan's other chores included feeding and combing the cows. Once in a while when he walked into the barn, his Grandpa Richard surprised him by squirting him with fresh milk straight from the udder.

On weekends Jordan and his dad, Jeff, would drive their white diesel pickup truck to Jordan's basketball games. Their pregame ritual was to pick up three or four 20-ounce bottles of Mountain Dew and drink them all on the way. Though according to the younger Zimmermann it bordered on addiction, those clear green plastic bottles always had him ready at jump ball.

For all its endearing qualities, life in a small Midwest town could get a little boring. So one day during senior year of high school, Jordan and his friends took a cue from the movie *Dazed and Confused*, hopped into a pickup truck, and started throwing water balloons all over the mall parking lot. To save Zimmermann's best tosses for his next start, they fashioned a balloon launcher that could clear a Subway or a Payless Shoes with no problem. There was a problem, however, when the police officer who pulled over Jordan and his friends explained how his wife was soaking wet from a direct hit.

With small town hijinx behind him and a baseball career in front of him, Jordan Zimmermann got to show his true heartland heart. Getting ready for junior year at Stevens Point, the baseball team was playing indoors to get out of the Wisconsin cold. Zimmermann's pitch was lined back to the box. Under the sterile fluorescent lighting, reaction time was nearly nil, and the ball broke Zimmermann's jaw. A couple of weeks later, with two steel plates and eleven screws holding his chin together like an old chicken coop, Jordan Zimmermann was back on the mound. He went 10-0 that season.

Sitting in the Hotel Bethlehem, Jordan Zimmermann doesn't seem burdened by the pressures of rescuing a Major League team from freefall. He is relaxed and composed as he predicts that a few days later he'll throw his first pitch down the middle for a strike and go about seven innings.

We are not surprised when on April 20 at Nationals Park, Zimmermann goes six innings in the rain for a 3 -2 win over the Atlanta Braves, the phenom's only critical mistake a fastball over the plate and a little up to Matt Diaz for a two-run homer.

The most significant thing to come out of Washington D.C. recently is a stimulus package. Fittingly, Washington has just received a stimulus package of its own.

"Movin' on up."

DONTRELLE'S ROAD BACK

May 4, 2009

Anyone who hasn't experienced some sort of anxiety lately may not have a beating heart. Between swine flu, the economy, and North Korea's missile test launch, to breathe is to worry. An anxiety *disorder*, however, is something else—anxiety triggered by any number of factors that can cripple one's ability to perform.

Dontrelle Willis was diagnosed with an anxiety disorder at the end of spring training. The diagnosis was based at least in part on the results of blood tests which indicated particularly high levels of certain hormones associated with stress. There was probably a lot more involved, not the least of which was Willis's ballooning ERA the past couple of seasons. But for a variety of reasons ranging from privacy to the insurance the Detroit Tigers took out a while ago on the lefty pitcher's $29 million three-year salary, the exact nature of the disorder is shrouded in layers of mystery not seen since J.R. was shot on a season-ending episode of *Dallas*.

So we did a little investigating of our own in the most enjoyable way we know how—by going to Willis's rehab start Friday night at Coca-Cola Park in Allentown, where the Toledo Mud Hens were in town to face the IronPigs. The very first thing we noticed about Dontrelle was his body language.

While he used to look like he was having fun out there, his high energy level was definitely toned down. Where Willis once combined shadows of the exuberance and herky-jerkiness exhibited more than three decades ago by that other Detroit Tigers man-child--the late Mark "The Bird" Fidrych—on Friday night Willis gave the shrugs and grimaces of a frustrated triple-A pitcher.

Most telling was the absence of his trademark high right leg kick. Against some batters on certain pitches, the kick vanished entirely. Willis's front foot would lift perhaps six inches off the mound, giving the appearance of almost dragging. It was as if Dontrelle was trying to tame his own baseball bronco and going about it all wrong. Against other batters, the leg went up in varying degrees. But even when the kick was back in height, it was not there in spirit. Compared to the 2003 NL Rookie-of-the-Year kick that helped the Florida Marlins win a World Series Championship against the Yankees, it had the look of a prosthetic limb.

Which is not to say Dontrelle Willis wasn't effective. He looked good striking out Andy Tracy and John Mayberry Jr., two skilled hitters in the heart of the IronPigs order. He threw more strikes than balls and followed the fastball with the change for good results. He worked out of a jam in the third inning that for a moment or two looked like it was going to be his unraveling. With over seven thousand fans in attendance watching Willis's every move, he didn't perform like someone with an anxiety disorder.

The truth about Dontrelle Willis may be somewhat simpler. His fastball averaged in the mid-80s Friday night, with a few topping out around 88 mph—three or four mph slower than the fastball that helped propel him to 22 wins and a near Cy Young Award in 2005. IronPigs designated hitter Mike Cervenak looked like he owned Willis, and when Dontrelle left his fastball up, Andy Tracy, John Mayberry Jr., and Jason Donald seemed to be taking extra batting practice licks. Willis also appeared a bit overweight, and that can't be helping.

When we caught up with Dontrelle during spring training in Lakeland, Florida, he was sitting in the clubhouse sneezing and visibly distressed. Still, he took the time to talk, accepted an invitation to participate in our next book project, and even disregarded every agent and team official's advisory by giving us that single most cherished piece of information—his cell phone number. And when we tried to shake his hand, he considerately reminded us he had a cold.

This is the same Dontrelle Willis who became the thirteenth ever African American pitcher to win twenty games in a Major League season and who, as Mudcat Grant's protégé, met with the President at the White House three years ago. Willis, like the nation, may be suffering from a confusing crisis of both ability and confidence, not knowing precisely where one ends and the other begins. We hope, as a very wise president said many years ago, Willis's real nemesis is only fear itself.

MANNY BEING NANNY

May 11, 2009

We knew LA was a little weird, but we really had no idea. Not even a year out there and sweet old Manuel Ramirez from the Bronx is caught taking human chorionic gonadotropin, a female fertility drug. Soon, Manny will be studying Kabbalah, eating quiche, and opening a Botox clinic in Malibu.

This wasn't exactly juicing. Let's call it milking. There are boobs and there are man boobs. Now there are Manny boobs. First there was Octo-mom. Now there's Octo-Manny. This is not Manny being Manny. This is Manny being Mommy. Just in time for Mother's Day. And this Mother's Day, Mom got a hypodermic needle and a syringe.

This is not so much a fifty-game suspension as it is a maternity leave. Sure we're disappointed. In breastfeeding terms, it's a real let-down. This will give a whole new meaning to the phrase "nursing an injury." But Manny doesn't need surgery. Manny needs a baby shower.

It's funny, Manny wasn't even showing. Too bad baseball isn't bigger over in Sweden, where this sort of thing is covered by medical insurance. But even as Chrysler files for bankruptcy, America remains a great innovator. Manny will be the first Major Leaguer to file a paternity suit against himself.

No doubt fifty games is a long time, almost two menstrual periods. That's enough time to shoot a pilot for an exercise show with Richard Simmons. It's enough time to do a cameo on *Desperate Housewives*, appear as a guest on *The Today Show* with Kathy Lee, and go on *The*

View. By July, Manny's baseball skills may have eroded, but he'll come back a better wet nurse.

Reintegrating Manny with the Dodgers after seven weeks won't be easy. First, there's the postpartum depression. Just ask Brooke Shields. That's right, we don't care what that Scientologist kook Tom Cruise says. When a power hitter comes back from maternity leave, there will be tears, and not just from fourth outfielder Juan Pierre, who will be riding the bench again. The returning slugger is liable to cry at any little thing, including the seven million dollars in contract payments he forfeited by fattening up like a turkey before slaughter.

But there is a bigger issue here than one man's love affair with cellulite. Bigger than one hombre's brave quest to morph into a strange hybrid of Rosie O'Donnell, Jennifer Lopez, and Michael Jackson. Just when we were getting used to the idea of a generation of ballplayers using performance enhancing substances, here comes this dude in dreadlocks taking performance *retarding* substances.

Frankly, it will be hard to look at all those 40-homerun seasons and not think somewhere in the back of our minds they were really 50-homerun seasons. By now, Manny could have passed the likes of Palmeiro, Sosa, and McGwire on the all-time doped-up dingers list. But alas, sometimes life just isn't fair. Ted Williams, Joe DiMaggio, Hank Greenberg, and Ralph Kiner had World War II. Manny Ramirez had progesterone.

Moreover, we remember a simpler time, when overpaid athletes shot their buttocks full of steroids and lied about it at Congressional hearings. When America's pastime meant sticking your teammates in the shower and watching your head blow up like a flesh balloon. When our sports heroes looked like Lou Ferrigno in an episode of *The Incredible Hulk* and got busted for beating the daylights out of a retired postal worker at a fender-bender. When José Canseco was the conscience of our nation.

Manny has taken all that away. Thanks to Manny Ramirez, real baseball played by real men on real steroids is just a mammary. From now on, even our asterisks will need asterisks.

"Manny being a Dodger."

"MICKEY MANTLE'S" IS A HOME RUN

May 18, 2009

Because we're sort of in the book business, people hand us books all the time to review. All too often our "review" consists of placing the volume on a large stack reserved for summer reading. We're just not sure which summer. Once in a while, however, a book comes along that never makes it to the pile because it's too good to put down.

"Mickey Mantle's," by William Liederman (The Lyons Press, 2007), never made it to the pile. Ostensibly, the book is a collection of stories relating to the author's nearly twenty years as owner and operator of America's most famous sports bar. It is that, but also a whole lot more.

When self-styled New York restaurateur Liederman has the idea in the late '80s to open up Mickey Mantle's, no one else believes a hard core sports bar can make it on posh Central Park South. No one, it turns out, except Mickey Mantle. Mickey and pal Billy Martin had lived in the St. Moritz Hotel in the 1950s right next door, when the same space was called Harry's Bar. Mickey and Billy were in Harry's Bar so often they called it Mickey's Place, and now thirty years later it really was.

You get a fair number of the drinking stories as well as the inside dirt you might expect from a book like "Mickey Mantle's". There are wayward ex-Yankee Joe Pepitone and boxing expert Bert Sugar, who never under any circumstances pay for a drink or a meal. There is belligerent, foul-mouthed Reggie Jackson whom no one has the guts to confront. There is the heroic side of Mickey Mantle who, pushing sixty years of age, straightens out a maniac stalking one of the waitresses.

There is even a bizarre tale of Muhammad Ali, already suffering from Parkinson's syndrome, visiting the kitchen staff and levitating himself several inches off the floor. Skeptical as we are, Liederman swears Ali did it without the help of ropes or countertops, because the owner himself was watching closely from just a few feet away.

But the real miracle of Mickey Mantle's was that it survived even half as long as it did. Liederman does an unparalleled job of describing the absolute impossibility, heartache and frenzy of running a large, well known eating and drinking establishment anywhere, let alone in that high-rent district, bureaucratic city of dreams and nightmares known as New York.

Cranking out sentences so long and breathless they seem to be run-on even though they are not, Liederman takes us round and round the revolving door of managers, chefs, waiters, waitresses, and bartenders who arrive at Mickey Mantle's with a drug, alcohol, or mental problem and leave—sometimes only days later—with an employment problem to boot.

For pure irony, it's hard to beat the tale of One-Tooth Tony. One-Tooth Tony occupies the pavement in front of Mickey Mantle's, lending Central Park South the flavor of Bowery and Canal Street. When Liederman finds himself understaffed in the dishwashing department, he tries to kill his entrepreneurial and altruistic urges with one stone by bringing One-Tooth Tony in off the streets. As much as he reeks and as much leftover food as he gloms, it is One-Tooth Tony who declares himself a free agent at the end of a single shift to return to his spot in front of Mantle's, where the pay is better and the corporate structure less demanding.

The walk-off home run of "Mickey Mantle's," however, arrives in October 2004, after the Red Sox achieve the most unforgettable comeback in professional sports history by beating the Yankees in four straight after falling behind three games to none in the American League Championship Series. Distraught his favorite team has been embarrassed, and even more so that the playoff cash spigot at the bar is effectively shut by the upset, Liederman temporarily converts Mickey Mantle's into Ted Williams's. It is a prank the owner believes the Mick appreciates from his watering hole in the Great Beyond and that regulars will recognize as a fitting gesture of comical mourning.

Liederman's miscalculations regarding the prank are epic and even land him and his family in hiding due to death threats. Though he lives on to write a singularly entertaining book, it is touch and go for a while.

Like all really good baseball books, "Mickey Mantle's" is more about the mad swirl surrounding the game—and life itself—than it is about hitting a round ball with a round bat. And for those of us who ever considered opening up a little place of our own, it is an effective cautionary tale.

"The Mick and the Bill."

LIDGE ON A RIDGE

May 18, 2009

Perfection is a dangerous concept. Perfection has often destroyed those who sought it. Among the few who have attained it, still more fell by the wayside trying to repeat it.

Closer Brad Lidge achieved a kind of perfection during the 2008 baseball season. By saving forty-one games in forty-one save opportunities and continuing that streak during the postseason to help the Phillies win their first World Championship in twenty-eight years, Lidge not only wrote himself into the history books but set a standard that may at some distant point be matched, but will never be exceeded.

The prospect of repeating such perfection died very early in the new season. Lidge has clearly struggled at points during the first month or so of the 2009 campaign, posting an earned run average over 8.00. But if you know anything about Brad Lidge, you know the struggle itself is what makes him tick.

It wasn't always that way. Lidge barely made his freshman and sophomore teams at Cherry Creek High School in Englewood, Colorado. As a free-spirit of the Great American West, he enjoyed hiking and cliff diving as much as baseball. On the diamond, he was an outfielder with a decent arm. He could also hit a little. But Cherry Creek's varsity team was perennially loaded with future Division I players and early round Major League draft picks.

As a junior on the JV squad, Lidge was asked to start a game as pitcher. He accepted the offer but then realized he had left his uniform home that day. So Lidge's would-be debut as a hurler was spent collecting splinters. When several games later Lidge remembered his uniform and took the mound, his 83-mile-per-hour fastball got him only so far. As the bases filled, the novice became rattled and threw hitter's pitches that only made the situation worse.

Cherry Creek JV catcher and future big leaguer Josh Bard expected more spine from the lanky right-hander and approached the mound. Removing his mask and standing face to face, Bard told Lidge he had to find a way to be mentally tough in these very situations if he was ever going to become a real pitcher.

Lidge took the words to heart and to mind. He had the DNA and life experience to do both. His father, Ralph Lidge Jr., was a law student turned real estate broker who always reasoned things out with his son. He and Brad's mom, Deborah, preferred mental over physical discipline and instilled in their son the idea that you could only truly improve anything about your own makeup by willing it yourself.

That included the physical aspects of life. When Brad was about twelve, he and his dad were hiking in Colorado. By putting one foot in front of the other for about eight hours, they finally reached a 14,000-foot peak. Amidst the lightheadedness and shortness of breath that accompanies such a thin atmosphere, the two prepared to descend.

But a large rock Brad stepped on flipped over and pinned his left leg to the ground. The five or ten minutes he was trapped tested his will to live and his ability to fight pain. After some passersby helped the Lidges, there was still the long perilous walk back down the mountain on a crushed leg and a lot of time to think about healing.

The summer between his junior and senior years, Brad Lidge went out every day by himself to a nearby ball field and practiced long toss. Some days he noticed an extra five or even ten feet of distance beyond his throws the previous day. By the end of the summer, Lidge would stand at home plate and throw the ball on a fly fifty feet past the left field fence into a sea of weeds.

On the mound, Lidge enjoyed a senior year that was literally out of left field and went on to a successful college career at Notre Dame. But the rocks had just begun rolling for Brad Lidge, who after being drafted in the first round by the Houston Astros in 1998 underwent four surgeries in three years and still more ups and downs after that.

To this day, Brad Lidge tells us, he still has no feeling along the inside of his left calf. What he does have are intense feelings for the game and for life. For those who think Lidge's perfection is behind him, think again. No one is better prepared mentally for the upcoming dog-day months of the season. That's a different form of perfection, and ultimately a more durable one.

"Lidge and BEST scholarship recipient Anthony Serrano"

THE PRICE IS RIGHT

May 25, 2009

The way it's supposed to be in baseball is you toil for years, finally make it to the postseason, and then reel off a bunch of quotes for the reporters about how sweet the promised land is. But a few players have entered Major League baseball in a Bizarro World where they land in the playoffs or World Series practically before their minor league suitcase is unpacked.

Todd Worrell comes to mind. With only 21-2/3 innings of Major League experience under his belt in 1985, he tamed the Dodgers and the Royals in postseason play, only to begin his "rookie" year the following April.

Left-handed pitcher David Price of the Durham Bulls may be Todd Worrell squared. When we spoke with Price this past Friday at Coca-Cola Park in Allentown, he was preparing to face batters the following night with names like Newhan, Donald, and Marson. Last October on national TV as a member of the Tampa Bay Rays, he faced a bunch of guys named Ortiz, Pedroia, and Youkilis and got them out en route to a win, a save, and trip to the World Series against the Phillies. In the Fall Classic Price put in two more impressive relief outings. All this without ever acquiring either a win or a save in a regular season Major League game.

But Friday night in Allentown, six-foot-six left-hander David Price was unfazed by the recent turn of events in his life. The way he explained it, facing the triple-A Phillies in May was as important as facing the big league Phillies in October. It was all a learning experience, and a pitcher who lacked the tools to struggle effectively lacked the tools to succeed. Price struggled with control of his 97 mph fastball in spring training and was sent back to the farm to work it out.

We got the sense that he would. At twenty-three, Price appears physically similar to a young David Justice, who always seemed pretty cool. In fact, Justice was Price's favorite player growing up in Tennessee, where TBS was a fixture in every home. Price tells us he remained a loyal Atlanta Braves fan right up until June 7, 2007, which happened to be draft day.

Price studied math and sociology at prestigious Vanderbilt University. He comes off as genuine and sincere and not at all a worrier. A signing bonus of $5.6 million as the first pick overall might do wonders for anyone's ability to remain calm during a demotion, but Price's serenity is priceless. He told us about his very first paycheck as a teenage umpire in a Pee Wee baseball game in his hometown of Murfreesboro. Price noticed the three-foot-nine right fielder was doing a real "pee dance," crossing his legs and bouncing around.

Umpire Price thought about stopping the game on some sort of urinary mercy rule, but with only one out that wasn't feasible. The next pitch was bounced to the infield, but it was the right fielder who cut loose, relieving himself on the outfield grass with the urgency of a kindergartener on a mission. Not only was it the funniest thing Price could ever recall seeing, he was also paid fifteen bucks for working the game.

With a lot more than fifteen dollars to manage these days, David Price takes the task as seriously as he takes the Saturday start against the IronPigs. Price and his father manage Project One Four (14 is Price's uniform number), which supports safety and athletic opportunity for kids from his neck of the woods. It is only at the end of our meeting, while discussing the foundation, that Price reveals the truly hard breaks in his life. In the past two years, he has lost his two best friends to accidents.

Knowing everything that David Price brings to the mound, we were as pumped for Saturday's game as we ever have been for a triple-A contest. At the last minute, however, he was scratched. We combed through our notes and made every conceivable conjecture but the right one—that David Price was called back up to the show. He is the likely starter for the Rays tonight against the Cleveland Indians. Fortunately, Price has all the postseason experience he needs to thrive in the regular season.

"Priceless."

FOR WHOM THE BELL TOLLS

June 1, 2009

Dreaded West Coast swings have been a nemesis for East Coast baseball teams ever since DC-8s full of Major Leaguers started crisscrossing the country in the late 1950s. The swing the Phillies begin tonight is no exception. The four games at Chavez Ravine against the streaking first place Dodgers is an obvious reason. But the opening series against the San Diego Padres is no mere warm-up.

In their 40th anniversary season, the Padres—who have yet to win a World Series—are no pushovers. Adrian Gonzales has 20 homeruns and is quietly decimating National League pitching. The one two punch of starting pitchers Jake Peavy and Chris Young can dominate a short series. And though San Diego is around a .500 team overall at the moment, their record at Petco Park is frightening 17-6.

No small part of the credit goes to closer Heath Bell. When the Padres let all-time great closer Trevor Hoffman go as a free agent, their set-up man made parting slightly less sorrowful. Over the previous two seasons Bell had appeared in an astronomical 155 games and produced enough holds to try professional wrestling. This year, Bell and Hoffman have been quietly competing for the Brad Lidge award. Prior to getting knocked around by the Rockies Saturday night, Heath Bell had saved 14 games in 14 opportunities, allowing a grand total of one run in 20 appearances.

The beginning for Heath Bell was not so auspicious. Growing up in the Los Angeles area, he was selected in 1997 by the Tampa Bay Devil

Rays in a draft round we weren't sure existed—the 69th. Bell stayed in Santiago Canyon College and the following year as an amateur free agent received an offer from the Mets for $500, a lot less than what a top closer makes for throwing a single pitch. It was Bell's sister Heather who convinced him to return the phone call.

It wasn't the first cue he took from a family member. Heath's dad was a marine. In boot camp one time, the drill sergeant brought in a marathon runner and told his men to follow the guy in the shorts until they dropped. The marines had a marathon in mind, but they weren't so lucky. This particular drill was more like several trips to Athens and back. At the end of 16 hours, the only men standing were the marathoner and Heath Bell's dad.

In the Mets system, Heath Bell's mentor was John Franco, the all-time left-handed leader in saves. Franco's version of reality was that twenty or thirty guys were trying to take his job and that every year he was getting older while they were getting younger. Bell was one of those wannabes, and Franco wasn't going to cut his protégé any slack.

Today, Heath Bell cuts no slack whatsoever to any competitor. When we caught up with him in Philadelphia during the Padres April trip east, he explained his one-man scouting system. A few days prior to a series he scans the cable and satellite TV. From the clubhouse, bed, bath, or weight room, Bell watches every swing of every hitter to see what they like, what they don't like, and especially if there is a hole in their plate coverage.

On game day, Bell fine-tunes his "book" on each player by watching the opposing team take batting practice. By the time his turn comes in the ninth inning, he has the hitter's strike zone scoped out like The Terminator.

But then, Bell tells us, something else takes over. After throwing the first meticulously thought out first pitch and having seen the batter react in the here and now, the closer shifts to an in-the-moment mentality, where the book in his brain hooks up to the fire in his gut. Bell goes after hitters with a pure overhand 97 mph fastball nipping least favorite corners in unpleasant sequence.

When the last pitch is thrown, Bell instantly transforms from stoic marine machine to wild child, complete with bouncing and fist pumping. To opponents it can be an annoying spectacle, but there doesn't seem to be an ounce of insincerity in it. It's just the expression of preparation having paid off. So unless the Phillies have studied Bell like Bell has studied them, it's going to be a long road trip.

"Bell and Bill."

JIMMY'S (ALMOST) BACK

June 8, 2009

The Phillies are in first place, and we're hearing a lot of complaints from Phillies fans. These two facts are not contradictory. The laments coming out of the City of Brotherly Love are about as surprising as homeowners griping about property taxes. What *is* relatively new are the great expectations. A string of good years, a World Championship, and being the team to beat will do that to a city.

In fairness, it is painfully obvious that the Phillies are running on five or six cylinders right now. Even a neutral observer has to wonder what kind of juggernaut the team would be on all eight cylinders. Lidge has gone from a lock to a liability, but the movement on his pitches is promising. Moyer, Blanton, and Hamels have started to turn it around. You know Ryan Howard will be heating up some more in July.

And then there is Jimmy Rollins. Arguably one of the five best five-tool players in the game, it took J-Roll most of April to cross to the high side of the Mendoza line. He got almost halfway back to .300 in May and then started fading again. His power and speed numbers are way down. Rollins's bat is a small fraction of a second behind the fastball, making line drives rarer.

Well, you Phanatics can stop worrying. When we caught up with Jimmy Rollins recently he was as cool as Shaft and focused as Kobe. He's not particularly worried, and given his personal history he has no reason to be.

Rollins's defense has remained crisp throughout his offensive slump. That is a reliable sign of commitment and professionalism. The defensive skills are ingrained in Jimmy. He learned them from his mom, Gigi, who was a top second baseman in softball leagues while Rollins was growing up in Alameda, California. Gigi played competitively right up through her son Jimmy's stint in the Phillies minor league system. According to J-Roll, Gigi still considers herself the better infielder.

Jimmy's younger brother, Antwon, played outfield with Encinal High School while Jimmy played shortstop. Together they won a city championship and led Encinal to a top-25 national ranking. Jimmy was drafted in the second round by the Phillies in 1996, and in 1998 Antwon was drafted in the fourth round by the Texas Rangers.

The way Jimmy sees it, Antwon had the better bat, more power, and more speed. But the reason Jimmy made it all the way up to the show and then some was love of the game. Antwon rarely enjoyed shagging fly balls, but you had to drag Jimmy off the field. That became a huge factor later on. As Jimmy tells us, "When you go from playing two or three games a week to playing a game every single day, you learn pretty fast if this is what you want to do with your life."

As a fourteen-year-old, Jimmy Rollins learned to cut hair. His father, Big Jim, and mother Gigi funded the start-up operation with a $16.99 pair of clippers from Walgreens. Brother Antwon was Jimmy's first "victim," as he puts it, and he went on to style scalps all over the Buena Vista Apartments. No longer needing any kind of an allowance gave Jimmy a sense of really contributing to his family for the first time.

But the most formative work experience for young Jimmy Rollins was his summer job with Operation Clean Streets. When Big Jim first got him the job, Jimmy wasn't thrilled. Pulling weeds from sidewalk joints in run-down West Oakland seemed thankless and endless. And while picking up clumps of litter was not an attractive task to begin with, there was an added hazard. The first day on the job, Jimmy was told to poke carefully at any garbage before applying pressure in case there was a dirty needle hidden within.

Somewhere around week two of Operation Clean Streets, Jimmy passed by one of the blocks he and his peers had tackled. The improvement in cleanliness, overall appearance, and even atmosphere on the block was palpable. From that moment on, Jimmy and friends went at it twice as hard, even bringing additional blocks into the program.

In the job he has now, Jimmy Rollins is counted on, looked up to, and well paid. As the long season progresses, his desire will only intensify. And there's one more thing. Take a look at Jimmy's face after gunning down a runner with a balancing-act throw on a play deep into the hole at short. That there is what you call a smile. And it's here to stay.

"Hot commodity."

1993 REDUX

June 15, 2009

The Phillies' mid-to-late June schedule looks like the team was dropped into the AL East and left there. But tomorrow's night's series opener at Citizens Bank Park against the Toronto Blue Jays holds special nostalgic significance.

A lot has happened since the 1993 World Series, including two controversial presidential administrations, two recessions, a bunch of wars and skirmishes, and the birth of the internet as we know it. Lenny Dykstra is known primarily as an investor. There are no players remaining from either roster. But the Blue Jays, as then, are managed by Cito Gaston.

Back in the day, Gaston set the standard for managerial excellence. In his first five seasons at the helm of the Toronto expansion franchise, his team finished first four times and won two World Series, in 1992 becoming the first—and still only—African-American to do so. Gaston never lobbied for the job. In fact, when Jimy Williams was fired in 1989, Gaston told the Toronto front office he preferred to remain as hitting coach. But Blue Jay players—with names like McGriff, Gruber and Olerud—told their coach he was their pick as manager, too.

When we caught up with Gaston earlier in the year, we understood the popular acclaim. The six-foot-four original member of the San Diego Padres carries himself like an international ambassador for the game, but an eminently approachable one. He told us receiving the Jackie Robinson Award for career achievement last year was right up there with either World Series ring.

Gaston talked about his manager on the Padres, the recently passed lifetime baseball journeyman Preston Gomez, as being a father to him. But Gaston credits his old roommate with the Atlanta Braves, Henry Aaron, with teaching him how to be a man. And ultimately it was Aaron who convinced Gaston to get back into baseball after his playing career never fully blossomed.

In his second stint with the Jays, Cito Gaston helped turn the team around, posting a 51-37 record in the second half of 2008 and nearly overtaking the Yankees for third place in the tough AL East. Some credit is due to the man who rehired Cito Gaston, Toronto Blue Jays General Manager J.P. Ricciardi.

When we ran into J.P. during spring training, what we saw was a casually dressed, forty-something athletically built man darting around foul territory during batting practice. We committed the faux pas of a lifetime in asking him if he was the clubhouse guy. We knew we were in trouble when before correcting us, he repeated our question to one of his subordinates, an assistant GM who laughed long and hard with his boss.

Juan Pedro Ricciardi played ball at Saint Leo University and was a Mets farmhand for a short while. He became a scout with the Yankees and A's organizations and went on to become an integral part of Billy Beane's maverick front office in Oakland. The A's specialized in getting the most out of a small payroll, revolutionized the way baseball statistics are used, and earned a reputation for late-season surges.

J.P. told us the his Toronto team, the one that posted the best ERA in the American League last year and an 86-76 record despite nary a player with more than 20 homeruns, has a philosophy. The philosophy is to play hard but stay loose. To have fun out there. That approach was evident from the body language of the players around us, from the manager, and by the fact that J.P. asked for a signed copy of our book for his sons instead of booting us from the team's complex in Dunedin.

The 2009 Phillies will have their hands full this week when they host J.P., Cito, and the Blue Jays. Though cooled off following their blazing start in April, the Jays are still knocking at the door in the AL East. Names like Scutaro, Lind and Hill provide low-cost, high octane fuel for a lineup that includes veterans like Kevin Millar and ex-Phil Scott Rolen.

The Phillies have already caught a break. Workhorse superstar pitcher Roy Halladay, 10 and 1 in the early going, has a pulled groin and will miss Wednesday's start. But the Phils face the Jays again at the end of the month in Toronto. With three games in Philadelphia and three games north of the border, it's almost 1993 all over again

"Henry Aaron's protégé."

GIVE KYLE KENDRICK
A REAL CHANCE

June 22, 2009

Perhaps it is Kyle Kendrick's quiet, easygoing demeanor that makes him the potential victim of practical jokes. There was the now almost legendary gag in the Phillies clubhouse during spring training 2008 when Brett Myers and a few other teammates informed Kendrick he had been traded to Japan for Kobayashi Iwamura, a fictitious player named after the hot dog eating champ Kobayashi. Kendrick swallowed the prank almost as fast as Kobayashi before Meyers informed him that he had been punked.

Kendrick was punked again on Friday, June 12 of this year when he was inserted into the 12th inning of a 2-2 ball game between the Phils and the Red Sox. A hard RBI single in the 13th by Jacoby Ellsbury opened the door to a three-run Boston inning and a loss for Kendrick and the Phillies.

But that was just the setup. Immediately following the game, the Phillies sent Kyle Kendrick back down to the triple-A Phillies affiliate in Allentown, where the right-hander had spent virtually all of the 2009 season to date. His task during those two-and-a-half months was to develop a changeup and cutter to go with his effective sinker.

The difference between getting punked by Ashton Kutcher and by a big league front office is how you feel afterwards. After Ashton—or Brett Myers for that matter—you are relieved, whether or not you are a reliever. But when you're a starter with a solid Major League track record who has just spent almost half a season fine-tuning your craft down on the farm, and your entire chance to prove yourself boils down to a late six-out appearance in a nail-biter, the ill effects could last a while.

In Kyle Kendrick's case, fortunately, they did not. The following Wednesday Kendrick threw a gem of a start in Durham, North Carolina against the Bulls, allowing no runs, four hits, and two walks in six sharp innings. No doubt the Major League Phillies could have used a start like that one while they were getting pounded by the Toronto Blue Jays.

When we spoke with Kendrick early in the current season, his mood was a little subdued. He knew in is heart he wasn't a triple-A pitcher, and Allentown was just a detour—two steps back before another three steps forward. Growing up in Mount Vernon, Washington, Kendrick excelled in baseball, football, and basketball. In 2003 he was offered a full ride and the quarterback position at Washington State University but signed with the Phillies instead after being drafted in the seventh round.

Kyle believed as a kid he was going to play in the big leagues, although he didn't know in exactly what capacity. His dad had been a shortstop in the Houston Astros organization, and Kyle played short in addition to pitching in Little League. He remembers the thrill of visiting Seattle's Kingdome in the mid-'90s, with its booming echo and the young Mariners on the rise. He absorbed some of Randy Johnson's go-get-'em attitude on the mound by osmosis, but Kendrick's man was Ken Griffey Jr., the dominant player of the era.

Kyle remembers sitting at home watching the 1995 playoffs against the Yankees. One time when Junior came around to score headfirst, Kyle's mom leaped straight up out of her seat. The combination of Mom's tall stature and the low ceiling led to a powerful collision between her arms and the drywall above. Kyle and his two brothers were doubly entertained.

Kendrick and his 93-mph sinker blitzed through the minors. He jumped from double-A Reading to the show in 2007, posting a 10-4 won-lost record and helping push the Phillies to a late season surge past the slumping Mets. Kendrick's high impact continued through the first two-thirds of the 2008 campaign, in which he went 10-5 before the National League hitters began catching up to him.

He was in uniform when the Phillies took it all last season and was thrilled when team president David Montgomery personally delivered Kendrick's World Series ring to Allentown along with those of IronPigs teammates Mike Cervenak and Andy Tracy. But Kendrick is in the middle of another battle right now—not the battle to get back to the Series, but the battle to get back his spot in the rotation.

He's getting closer. Since we spoke with Kendrick he has posted a 3.70 ERA in 13 starts in the competitive International League, surrendering only 74 hits in 72 innings and issuing only 23 walks. Right before every one of those starts, Kyle's father texts him the same message: "Be aggressive, have fun, and get ahead in the count." Kendrick has earned the chance to try that approach in the big leagues again. And not just for two innings.

"Kyle and fiancée Stephenie LaGrossa"

HALL OF FUN CLASSIC

June 29, 2009

In his 40s, pitching legend Bob Feller was clocked in the 90s. In his 90s, Feller has been clocked in the 40s, and the latter may be the greater accomplishment. To be precise, Feller is barely 90 and can probably bring it in the high 40s. The exact numbers didn't matter much on Father's Day, when Feller started for the Honus Wagner team in the Cooperstown Hall of Fame Classic.

We doubt the Elias Sports Bureau has statistics for the most senior pitcher to record an out in a Major League sanctioned old timer's game, but Rapid Robert surely entered the stratosphere when he got former All-Star Bobby Grich to ground out to first base. Feller had less luck with Hall of Famer Paul Molitor, who drilled a single. Two base knocks later, Feller was pulled from the game but was philosophical, saying he needed more outfielders—"about ten more." Fortunately, reliever, Hall of Famer Fergie Jenkins, got the Eddie Collins team to hit into a double play to keep Feller's Hall of Fame Classic ERA to a an even 27.00.

After years of struggling to schedule exhibition games between current Major League teams, the Hall of Fame tried something completely different this year. Hall of Fame President Jeff Idelson and Major League Baseball Players Alumni Association CEO Dan Foster staged the inaugural Classic as a feel-good event. It definitely felt good. Scenic Doubleday Field was packed with over 7,000 fans who came to see all-time greats like Brooks Robinson, Phil Niekro, and Lee Smith ply what is still left of their trades. They came to see recent retirees like

Jeff Kent and Steve Finley square off in a homerun derby and were not disappointed with the Ruthian blasts into the hills of Cooperstown.

They got to mill around in the autograph tent and the outskirts of the field, where some of the best Father's Day gifts you could ever invent were largely free and so was the conversation between baseball legends and everyday fantasy league enthusiasts. Along the sidelines of Doubleday Field, everyone from former Yankees outfielder Kevin Maas to local favorite Steve Grilli hung out telling stories, bringing back that long gone idyllic era when ballgames were played in town squares with no clear boundaries between player and fan.

Then Jon Warden got out there and things got a little funky. Warden pitched in 1968 for the World Champion Detroit Tigers and blew his arm out the following spring training. Since then he has made a name for himself as the funniest man in baseball not counting Roger Clemens's futile attempts to clear his name. Warden is king of the banquet circuit and runs a charity memorabilia auction like Robin Williams on caffeine.

Without the benefit of a microphone, Warden's verbal pyrotechnics might have suffered, but he made a transition to physical comedy that would have left Max Patkin smiling. Warden's "called shot" wound up as a weak dribbler toward the mound. When pitcher Fergie Jenkins ran toward the first base line to tag out the runner, Warden ably called "time out." Later in the game, Warden's act got a little less squeaky clean when he was spotted walking toward the batter's box with a long string of toilet paper trailing from his pants.

But, all in all, the game was no joke. A rocky first inning aside, the final score was 5-4. Though Brooksie didn't get the chance to levitate at the hot corner, numerous solid efforts in the field were highlighted by the terrific outfield play of former Red Sox pitcher Bill Lee. At a youngish 62, the "Spaceman" not only can still shag them but he collected two base hits as well. A quick look at the *Baseball Encyclopedia* demonstrates this was no fluke, as Lee hit .364 playing for the Montreal Expos in 1981, his last full year in the bigs. The former All-Star and still current cerebral hippie autographed a baseball "Bill Lee, Earth," indicating that the Spaceman's persona has settled down a bit even if his baseball skills have not.

The upstate New York rain held off except for about ten minutes, which in the land of countless soaked induction speeches and Woodstock was a blessing. Even that minor delay was compensated for by 283-game winner and longtime broadcaster Jim Kaat quick-pitching batter after batter and reminding us in the age of ten-minute at-bats of the joys of sub-two-hour games.

But this was a game we wanted to go on and on, and hopefully it will—next year and for many years to come. The first Hall of Fame Classic was exactly was what the name promised and did more for the game in seven innings than steroids testing and awkward press conferences could do in a lifetime.

"Roaring 90s"

NOT YOUR AVERAGE CATCHER

July 6, 2009

As summer goes into full swing, there is a swirl of political controversies, celebrity deaths, and sports tragedies. Even with the Los Angeles Dodgers, who travel east to face the Mets tomorrow, there are a pack of reporters and cameras following recently unsuspended superstar Manny Ramirez. Somewhere beneath the radar is a big reason the Dodgers have opened up a six-and-a-half game lead in the National League West and have the best record in baseball. His name is Russell Martin.

His full name is Russell Nathan Jeanson Coltrane Martin. It's no average name, and Martin is no average catcher. His dad, Russell Martin, was a successful running back and safety in college and was once cut by the Rough Riders of the Canadian Football League just before the regular season started. Jeanson is his mom, Suzanne's, last name. We're not sure where the Nathan comes from, but the Coltrane, now there's a story.

Martin's dad was a skilled jazz saxophonist who at one point made his living playing down in the Metro, Montreal's subway system. As an eight-year-old, Russell helped his father on some days count Loonies and Toonies (the Canadian nicknames for one- and two-dollar coins). While sorting change and adjusting a speaker here and there, young Russell got an education in the best jazz ever made—Duke Ellington, Ella Fitzgerald, Charlie Parker, and of course that shooting star sax master who left this Earth way too early, Russell's namesake, John Coltrane.

Were the story to continue like a simple arpeggio in G-minor, Russell Martin would have grown up eating quiche and opening up an eclectic record shop in Verdun. But Martin was a baseball player from day one. He followed the Expos and their stars—Tim Raines, Larry Walker, Andres Galarraga—and marveled at All-Stars stateside like the Wizard, St. Louis Cardinals shortstop Ozzie Smith. Martin took ground balls even in the cold Montreal winters and in pursuing his dream had to play a continual countermelody.

In Canada, all the kids were wrapped up in hockey. For two years Martin lived with his mom and step-dad in Paris, where all his peers cared about was soccer. Through the entire symphony of his youth, Martin was able to squeeze in a couple bars of *Take Me Out to the Ball Game* wherever they would fit. One summer, Russell's father even put together a baseball camp in Montreal so his son could come home from France for eight weeks, remember how to throw down to second base, and work off all those croissants.

Through those years of resolve, Russell Martin became a fighter, not so much in the pugilistic sense but in terms of his emotional makeup. He argued with his high school coach at Edouard Montpetite, also the alma mater of pitcher Eric Gagne. Martin wouldn't allow anyone to tamper with the swing he had developed watching the likes of Joe Carter on TV, and when Russell and his coach went at it verbally in hard core scatological French, Martin almost got kicked out of the program. In Paris on one occasion, it did get physical when Martin got into a kicking match with a French bully and wound up with sore shins for a year. Times like those, you wish you had the catcher's tools of ignorance.

Today, in his fourth year as starting catcher for the Dodgers, twenty-six year old Russell Nathan Jeanson Coltrane Martin is reportedly a more level-headed individual. His girlfriend, Marikym, has got him doing yoga and getting better rest. Martin isn't hitting for the kind of average and power he did in 2007, when he was a Silver Slugger, an All-Star, and a Gold Glove catcher to boot. But he is doing the quiet things a catcher must do to advance a team.

Using the musical and chart-memorizing tools he picked up north of the border, Russell Martin spends enormous amounts of time going over hitters' strengths and weaknesses and talking strategy with his pitchers. It must be working. The Dodgers staff—with rising stars like Billingsley, Kershaw and Broxton—has posted an ERA of 3.56, second only to the Lincecum-led San Francisco Giants. The Dodgers are the team to beat in the NL, and the Mets need them visiting Citi Field like they need David Wright joining the rest of his team on the DL.

But the true test of a player's personal progress comes at odd times. We were scheduled to speak with Russell Martin after a night game with the Phillies in mid-May. It so happened that on that night Jason Werth stole four bases off of Martin en route to a 5-3 win for the Phils. The worst of the carnage occurred in the seventh inning when Werth stole second, third, and finally home. There is nothing more embarrassing for a catcher. Not a passed ball. Not dropping an easy foul pop. Not throwing into centerfield. Nothing.

We weren't sure Russell Martin would make the interview. But a little before midnight at the Weston Hotel, the Dodger catcher walked out into the lobby with a smile on his face and a bunch of great stories to tell. He explained that he had just spent about an hour reviewing a video of Werth stealing home and had resolved from now till eternity to peek down the third baseline before throwing back to the mound, no matter how preoccupied he might be.

It seems living in Los Angeles agrees with Russell Martin.

"The catcher and Officer Scott Dempsey"

CITI FIELD IS A DIAMOND

July 13, 2009

Three months into the regular season and we were long overdue for the grand tour of the Mets' new home, Citi Field. Full disclosure—One of us grew up a couple of miles from Shea Stadium and for years worked right across Roosevelt Avenue in a barrack-like building for the New York City Department of Parks.

Shea itself had a barrack-like motif, and when you weren't watching the flight of the ball you could spend anywhere from a minute to an hour watching a hot-dog wrapper in the swirling wind spiral its way down to the infield. So even a seriously flawed replacement stadium would have passed for a big improvement.

But the new ballpark is more than a big improvement. It's a well executed combination of state-of-the-art amenities and classic architectural features. Whereas fans used to slip in to Shea unceremoniously through scattered turnstiles in a series of anonymous ground level portals, there is a single entrance to Citi Field. Located behind home plate, the Jackie Robinson Rotunda is essentially a separate structure, a massive brick-arched atrium with a hint of Ebbets Field.

As you ride up one of the escalators and take in the view of the ceiling that seems almost as high as the *Duomo* of Florence, Italy, you are also viewing a panorama of massive black and white photos of the rotunda's namesake, accompanied by the words of his timeless motto: "A *life is not important except in the impact it has on other lives.*" The atrium itself has a mighty impact, and for a moment you wonder why the entire stadium wasn't named for Robinson, until you remember this is corporate America.

Inside the ballpark even the most casual students of architecture will appreciate the raw steel support structure, visible just about everywhere. None of the busy rollercoaster patterns popularized in ancient parks like Griffith Stadium or Wrigley. The steel beams, girders, and arches at Citi Field are fewer and more elegant. Still, the stadium seems like it's been there a lot longer than it has.

The Mets' lack of power this season cannot be blamed entirely on the roster and its numerous injuries. Citi Field is not a hitter's park. The 384 feet to dead left field is made less surmountable by the high fences. In right field, 378 stretches out closer to 400 feet in a little cove prominently franchised by Modell's sporting goods. Strangely, the fences here transition higher, so that the only real Death Valley in New York is no longer in the Bronx. Even so, during our Wednesday night visit Manny Ramirez hit a solo homerun for the Dodgers in the top of the ninth inning to the right pocket of Modell's cove, though just barely.

The other prominent oddity of the field itself is not an obstacle for hitters but for outfielders. The wide tracts of land in foul territory shrink to about the width of a Smart Car toward the foul poles. This feature may be great for unruly fans looking to make their Major League debut, but it's less than ideal for a left- or right-fielder tracking down a fly ball drifting toward the line. The best slide stop in the world could still land a player on the DL with a pulled groin or bruised shin.

But why quibble? The press boxes are so far on the other end of the spectrum from the seedy Damon Runyon era facilities of yore you want to keep checking over your scorecard, schmooze and never go home. There are multiple large high-tech scoreboards and a series of long ribbon scoreboards at the base of the upper deck that add a festive, circus atmosphere.

The corridors are wide, and the temptations to leave your seat and wander many. Following in the new tradition of Camden Yards, the outfield is not a wasteland but a mall and marketing bonanza, ripe with opportunities to miss a few innings purchasing famous name sportswear. A steel truss bridge linking two different areas of the mall is perhaps the finishing touch.

But the most favorable improvement over Shea requires about half a game to dawn on you. The commercial jet planes headed for La Guardia continue to land just beyond the park every few minutes, alarmingly low and close. But whereas in Shea the sound of Rusty Staub lining a single to right was lost in a 105-decibel torrent, the sounds of baseball at Citi Field remain audible. This is largely the result of the seating and other structures that enclose Citi Field and make it a cozy setting. Sure beats looking at a parking lot and scrap yards.

"New field, old beer."

ANDY TRACY IS A ROCK

July 20, 2009

If he was twenty-five years old, he would have been called up by now.
So far this season at the Triple-A level, he's hit 15 homeruns, 19 doubles,
and knocked in 57 runs. He was named International League Batter
of the Week for June 15-21 and had 10 RBI during the span. He was
named to the I.L. All-Star team and hit five homeruns in the first round
of the Triple-A homerun derby in Portland, Oregon. As a power hitter,
he has even stolen five bases this year.

But Andy Tracy of the Lehigh Valley IronPigs is thirty-five. While
that's young for a mortgage broker, lawyer, reality television series star,
or politician, it's up there for anyone knocking on the door of the Major
Leagues. And when you're behind Ryan Howard on the depth chart at
first base, it can feel downright ancient.

None of this seems to bother Andy Tracy in the slightest. In fact,
he is so philosophical about his status in the game he could be mistaken
for a Zen Master. When we caught up with Tracy earlier in the season,
he laid it out straight: "I want the Phillies to know that I'm available.
I'm like an insurance policy with Ryan up there."

Tracy has a staggering 246 homeruns in the minor leagues, a total
to which he adds weekly. He is an acknowledged clubhouse leader and
one of the big reasons the IronPigs are still alive in the I.L. North race.
He is at a peak of sorts but not tooting his own horn.

There have been other peaks. Ten seasons ago, he was the talk of
Double-A. His monster year with Harrisburg of the Eastern League

included 37 homeruns and 128 RBI and led to a promotion with the Montreal Expos the following year. In 2000, Tracy had more than a cup of coffee in the show, playing first and third base and collecting a half season's worth of at-bats. He overcame knocking knees in his very first at-bat to single home a run, but a respectable .260 average and 11 homeruns did not earn him a coveted starting spot for the following season.

The peak of peaks, at least so far, came at the end of the 2008 season, when along with Mike Cervenak, Greg Golson, and Lou Marson, Tracy was called up to the World Series as a standby player. There were no knocking knees for Andy Tracy when he took batting practice at Citizens Bank Park. The way he explains it, after all the seasoning he doesn't get overly excited about much anymore. His main concern was getting in and out of the cage quickly so as not to mess up the routine of the active roster players.

The 2008 peak included winding up smack in the center of the celebration pile complete with wide smile in the *Sports Illustrated World Series Commemorative Edition*. Moments before the last out in the Game 5, which Tracy describes as comparable to sudden death in the final game of the Stanley Cup, he and his fellow call-ups threw modesty to the wind and decided to pile on as if they had played every inning. They knew they might never be there again, and knowing how to enjoy the moment is the other side of being philosophical. This spring, after receiving his championship ring directly from Phillies President David Montgomery, Tracy and his wife sat up half the night and talked about the long, strange journey and what it all meant.

The peak almost no one ever hears about, however, is Andy Tracy's 2007 season in New Orleans with the Zephyrs, the Mets' Triple-A PCL affiliate. Still in the aftermath of Hurricane Katrina, the team started the year by taking a tour of the ravaged neighborhoods and getting to know the residents. Playing third fiddle to the football Saints and basketball Hornets, the Zephyrs throughout the year reached out to the Boys & Girls Clubs and held as many events as possible at the field. But the first baseman knew residents had a lot more on their mind than going to a baseball game.

Reality for the Bowling Green, Ohio native—the youngest of eight kids—might eventually be coaching in the pros. The standard take is that Andy Tracy has the combination of communication skills and personal grit to become, one day, a successful manager. But reality for the moment is that from this point in the season through September, Major League Baseball is all about shrewd personnel moves, and the Phillies are among a long list of teams who need reliable power coming off the bench.

"Clubhouse casual."

PERFECT VIEW OF A PERFECT GAME

July 27, 2009

Thursday afternoon at Citizens Bank Park was shaping up to be a fairly routine day at the ballpark. It was getting near four o'clock. As Ryan Howard put on a one-man homerun derby, we rehearsed our questions: What has sparked the Phils in July? Any chance of snagging Roy Halladay before the trade deadline?

We had a list of questions for the visiting San Diego Padres, too. But as we looked over at the third base dugout, it was empty. Not empty as in a couple of lesser known players milling about and tinkering with equipment. Completely empty. Someone from security said Mark Buehrle of the Chicago White Sox was working the eighth inning of a possible perfect game.

Without further adieu, we hustled down the three steps, down the corridor, then up the six steps to the visiting clubhouse. Gathered around the ceiling-mounted TV in the middle of the expansive locker room were about twenty Padres. It is unlikely the Padres are going to the World Series this year, but from the atmosphere you'd have thought they were at least watching one.

The players quickly filled us in on the fourth inning Evan Longoria line drive right at White Sox shortstop Alexei Ramirez and the numerous less threatening ground balls throughout the game. Then, in our initiation, we watched the Pat Burell line drive to left. A bunch of big guys named Correia, Peavy, Mujica, Gwynn, and Giles in various states of undress held their collective breath. But the line drive, as so many smashes by Pat Burell do, curled foul.

At this point, an impromptu head count revealed just how many in the gathering were pitchers. Unlike President Obama, these players had no particular connection to the American League team from the Windy City. But they were not impartial observers of the game. They were, for the time being, the nation's number one fans of the workhorse lefty perennial All-Star from Chicago. Buehrle was clearly one of their own out there, a member of the brotherhood of the traveling pitch count. Each cutter or hook was one small toss for a man, one giant toss for hurlers everywhere.

Then came the play of the game, soon to be a YouTube classic. After being inserted as a ninth inning defensive replacement in centerfield by White Sox manager Ozzie Guillen, DeWayne Wise darted back on a fly ball hit a ton by Tampa Bay's Gabe Kapler. There were a series of successive yelps, booms and shrieks within the clubhouse sonar explosion that accompanied Wise's reach above the top of the wall, his snatch of the ball with a gloved right hand, his juggling of the ball into his bare left hand, and his final tumble to the sod. For a moment we were all watching Willie Mays robbing Vic Wertz in the 1954 Fall Classic. We were all a struggling platoon outfielder with a tremendous vertical leap saving the day for his team and for posterity.

The final out, a ground gall to shortstop Ramirez, brought not only group hugs, wicked high-fives, and some nearly damaged furniture. There was reflection on witnessing history. Closer Heath Bell gave kudos to Ozzie Guillen for a move so timely it seemed psychic. Starter Josh Geer talked about his own mercurial rise from Navarro Junior College, to Rice University, to the Padres staff where he is now fighting to keep his spot in the rotation. Geer remarked that a game like this was the ultimate affirmation that in baseball you just had no idea what might happen from one day to the next. Big stick Adrian Gonzalez, who enjoyed every out, said he never wanted to go down on the wrong side of history and wondered if he would do anything differently as a batter if ever faced with that situation.

Across the way, Phillies closer Brad Lidge recounted the game for the ages of which he was a part in 2003 in which six different Houston Astros pitchers no-hit the Yankees in Yankee Stadium. In that one, an

8-0 blowout in which starter Roy Oswalt went down with an injury, rookie Lidge was a middle reliever, and closer Billy Wagner eventually came in just to get his name in the books. That night, the phone in Lidge's hotel rang off the hook till five AM, and the young reliever and his wife realized why veteran players on the road check in under an alias.

By around six o'clock in the evening Thursday at Citizens Bank Park, the spontaneous festivities had died down. There was still a discernable buzz at field level from the notion that in baseball, as in life, indeed anything was possible. And for a couple of reporters there was the added afterglow of being simply a fan among fans who happened to wear a Major League uniform. But this glow, too, soon began to fade. We all had another ballgame to do.

THIRTY YEARS AFTER THURMAN

August 3, 2009

Thirty years ago this week millions of baseball fans were stunned by the tragic death of Yankees catcher Thurman Munson. One of us was a high school kid taking summer classes at Bucknell University in Lewisburg, Pennsylvania. The guy in the next dorm room didn't even like baseball but knew his neighbor was obsessed with the Yankees and knocked on the door with some news he had just heard on the radio. Thus began a frantic search across the AM dial. But as the young, displaced New Yorker failed to find a station that would retract or correct the story, he also had a strange, sinking sensation the '70s were over.

Marty Appel's book, *Munson: The Life and Death of a Yankee Captain*, published this summer by Doubleday, gives the once heartbroken fan a chance to relive not simply the fateful demise of the stalwart backstop three decades ago, but virtually the entire rise and fall of the 1970s New York Yankees. With the perspective of history there is not only the opportunity for some closure but also for revisiting the pure fun of following baseball in a simpler time.

As a member of the Yankees public relations department from 1968 to 1977, PR director for three of those years, and confidante of many players including Munson himself, Appel had better than a front row seat. He was a family member with an all-access pass. While reading *Munson*, one gets the feeling that Appel is doing more than just a splendid job relating stories and controversies of the Bronx Zoo and pre-Bronx Zoo eras. He is engaged in a catharsis of his own. The personal touch throughout might be a little sentimental for eternal fans of *Ball Four*, but for anyone who admired Thurman Munson, it is therapy.

Thurman Munson was a complex man. That his gruff mannerisms, particularly in dealing with the media, hid his depth as a person was no accident. Even a future baseball writer, as a carefree kid in the clubhouse, was hesitant to ask for his autograph. Munson's droopy mustache and predilection for plaid polyester pants did not exactly cast him as a man-about-town. But the Munson who remolded the once great but cellar dwelling Yankees in his own squat image and brought home two consecutive World Championships had issues larger than baseball on his mind.

Growing up had been challenging at best. His father, Darrell Munson, a working class guy, was Thurman's worst critic. Though not a heavy drinker himself, Darrell was the child of an alcoholic and seemed to pass down the severity and nastiness of that experience. Childhood friends paint Thurman, the youngest of four, as an afterthought. Worse, his father saw the young Thurman as more of a personal rival than a son, a particularly toxic environment for the formative years.

Aside from bringing a winner back to New York, not becoming a clone of his father was Thurman Munson's life work. Breaking the mold became a possibility when he met his high school sweetheart, Diana Dominick. Diana's family was a refuge for Thurman, and when the two started a family of their own, Tracy, Kelly, and Michael became everything. It was Thurman Munson's young family, in fact, and his disdain for being away, that drove him to purchase and fly faster and faster planes, allowing him to make quick flights home on getaway and off days.

Appel's chronicle of Thurman Munson's evolution to Yankee captain is probably the most joyful aspect of *Munson*. The story of the catcher in August 1970 driving up the New Jersey Turnpike on leave from Reserve duty in Fort Dix is oddly compelling. He arrives at dinosaur Yankee Stadium just in time to pinch-hit late in the second game of a double-header and line out to Brooks Robinson at third. Statistically, the moment means little in a season in which the surging Yankees fall short of a division title. But the appreciative reaction of the fans signals that a new era has begun for the previously downtrodden Bronx Bombers.

The legendary infighting between Munson, Reggie Jackson, Billy Martin, and George Steinbrenner is well traveled turf by now. Appel intelligently does not try to outdo *The Bronx is Burning*. Instead, a well placed story of Reggie and Thurman reconciled and flying on the catcher's new Cessna Citation offers more depth and nuance than a thousand tales of media sabotage ever could.

Literally the final one hundred or so pages of *Munson* cover the fateful crash at Akron-Canton Airport August 2, 1979 and the events surrounding it. The accounts are never quite graphic or macabre but nonetheless lend the reader the full sense of being there and devastated thirty years back in time. Detail of the close-knit nature of the Yankees, even as the team is being torn apart by personnel moves, is an effective antidote to the Bronx Zoo-like accounts of the period.

"Munson and Billy back in the day."

Still Wild About Harry

August 10, 2009

When a friend passes, there is a funeral service. There are obits, eulogies, and a swirl of activities that all seem to have one effect—not letting the passing sink in. The sinking in comes later, at odd moments.

When Phillies broadcaster and legend Harry Kalas passed away in April, we had our own recollections, of course. As a schoolteacher, one of us had applied last year to J-Roll's Aces on behalf of the Bethlehem Career Academy. BCA is a school for at-risk kids. J-Roll's Aces, Jimmy Rollins's program, gives underprivileged kids a chance to come out to the ballpark and get the red carpet treatment. The two programs seemed like a great double-play combination.

We received our twenty-five tickets for two adults and twenty-three kids. Chaperoning twenty-three fourteen-year-olds is never easy, but it's even harder when you're sifting through a crowd of thousands at Citizens Bank Park and your kids are all hyped up about meeting the reigning National League MVP. But there is no program for chaperones at risk, and so we made our way past the players' parking lot searching for the right entrance.

There, leaning against the fence, was Harry Kalas. There was no imposing on Harry. He was at least as ready to talk to us as we were to him. The kids didn't have on their J-Roll's Aces t-shirts, but no explanation was necessary. They were just kids coming to see a game, and by his accommodating nature Harry Kalas was the best unofficial ambassador a franchise ever had.

There was no introduction necessary for the kids, either, at least not after the first few seconds. The kids weren't all huge baseball fans, but the moment they heard the voice it was all over. The voice was gravelly, regal, distinct and the soundtrack of three generations. For one of the chaperones, the memory dated back to 1973 and being almost the same age, in the same position as these kids. Harry Kalas looked more like a kid himself then and wasn't a legend yet, but the voice and love for the fans were identical.

Over time, the voice became the soundtrack for hot summers by a TV with rabbit ears, when the first day of school was drawing too near but you didn't worry about it. Lefty, Michael Jack Schmidt, and Luzinski were surging toward a division title and maybe a pennant, and Harry Kalas and Richie Ashburn were going to be there with you every inning.

Back to 2008 near the players' parking lot, one of the kids asked Harry Kalas who his favorite Phillie was. There was no hesitation from the Ford C. Frick Award recipient. "J-Roll," Kalas said, "is a class act both on and off the field. He's what every baseball player should strive to be." Talk about authentic sounding. You could have dropped it right into a Campbell's Soup commercial.

Then a chaperone remembered a question of his own—would Harry Kalas consider doing a chapter for the next volume of *Before the Glory*? Up until that point, there had been plenty of great ballplayers but no broadcaster in the project, and who better to represent the profession than *our voice*? Harry smiled, took a copy of *Volume I* with the media kit, and said it would be his pleasure. We had high hopes.

Flash forward to the middle of the 2009 season. The chaperone is in the Phillies dugout with Jimmy Rollins before a game. We're reminiscing about Harry, and Rollins is talking about the plane rides. Harry was always one of the players. He sat in the back with J-Roll, Utley, Burrell, Lidge and the others. There was a thought of playing poker with the guys, but before long Harry just slept. He dozed with his briefcase through hundreds of hands of five-card draw, all sorts of scary turbulence, and even rough landings.

But on the flight to Washington D.C. in April, Kalas sat up front and J-Roll busted his chops for it. The broadcaster said his briefcase was getting a little heavy, and Rollins told him he'd better get his butt to the back just the same.

In the dugout, near the bat rack, the chaperone mentions that Rollins was Kalas's favorite player. Rollins stops talking and in dead silence stares out toward the field. There is a tear coming from the right eye of the game's scrappiest player. Then the shortstop explains. When he received a request from Harry's widow, Eileen, to be a pallbearer, Rollins assumed it was as a representative of the players. He had no idea, until that odd moment, what was behind the request. And for the chaperone and the shortstop, it finally sank in.

"Our sentiments exactly."

Baseball According to George Thorogood

August 17, 2009

We finally met our match. Thursday afternoon we got the call. George Thorogood was playing at the Count Basie Theater in Red Bank, New Jersey. We've been big fans for about thirty years and knew of Lonesome George's reputation as baseball fan extraordinaire. Using back channels, we had put in an interview request some time ago, and now we had exactly two hours to drop whatever we were doing and get on the Garden State. "And one more thing," George said. "Bring a pretty girl with you."

Cara Senese, a sharp schoolteacher from the Poconos, was our pretty girl. George Thorogood and his manager, Mike Donohue, were waiting for us in the tour bus parked outside the theater. George looked at us deadpan and began what we realized was something in between initiation and hazing. "Who," he asked, "in the history of the Yankees organization, had the longest unbroken tenure in the clubhouse?" It was not a player or manager, but rather Pete Sheehy, the clubhouse attendant whose reign spanned seven decades. A homerun for Billy's team, and with that we had walked our forty-seven miles of barbed wire and become instant members of George Thorogood's road crew.

It seems everyone knows George's reputation for booking concert tours around the baseball season. And many people are aware that back in the '70s he played second base in the Roberto Clemente League in

Delaware and was voted rookie of the year. But until you see Thorogood in action, you can't imagine what a baseball freak he really is. The heck with the pre-concert meet and greet and the sound check. With fresh blood on the bus to talk baseball, we thought sixteen hundred screaming rock and roll fans were going to be issued a rain check and come looking for us.

George is close friends with Bob Costas and explains that if Bob or anyone can't give him six solid hours to talk about the Babe, the Mick, and Joe D, it's better not to start. Among the thousands of stories the two aficionados have shared, George's favorite may be the time Ted Williams, Joe DiMaggio, Stan Musial, and Mickey Mantle wound up in the same hotel room talking about hitting. While Ted, Joe, and Stan the Man got pretty loud, Mickey was virtually silent. Finally, one of the three demanded to know what the switch-hitter thought. Whether it was his .298 lifetime batting average, respect for his elders, or just plain awe, Mantle looked around the room, shook his head, and walked out.

Lonesome George's favorite personal memories of the game surround the traveling old-timers game sponsored by Equitable Life. In 1986, he was asked to sing the National Anthem for the game in Denver. Thorogood is generally not the nervous type, but with folks like Fergie Jenkins and Bob Gibson looking on, George could have used a bourbon, a scotch, and a beer that day. When it came time to talk to Joe DiMaggio, George's throat was feeling mighty dry. Like Mickey, George's tongue was tied. The difference was, Thorogood approached DiMaggio again and asked for a second at-bat.

As George's tongue became untied, he noticed a bunch of fans down the third base line holding up a bunch of his albums and beckoning him to sign. Thorogood had a conflict—either disappoint his fans or cut out on the greatest living ballplayer. But Joltin' Joe gave him the nod. George belonged with his fans. So the bluesman moved it on over to the stands and signed until there was not an album cover or sleeve or stray program left. He couldn't disappoint Joe D.

The show Thursday night at the Count Basie Theater was what you would expect from GT and the Destroyers—two hours of rock and roll bedlam with two wild encores and no fanny ever firmly in a seat. Afterwards, George told us a story that had nothing to do with baseball.

It was the early '80s, and he was at the offices of *Rolling Stone*. Ever the rock fan, he wandered into the archives to pick up some classic editions of the magazine.

In the room were two slightly geeky librarian dudes who knew the archives like the back of their hands. Looking at George, they were awestruck, much like George looking at Joe D. And then Thorogood saw taped to the wall by their desks—out of all the Elvis, Hendrix, Lennon, Dylan, and Clapton covers in the room—was the *Rolling Stone* cover featuring George Thorogood. It was at that moment he understood his working man audience and bar-chorded it into his heart. And the moment we heard that one, we realized we had some other story to file this week—something about Pedro, or A-Rod, or Big Papi—but it would just have to wait.

"Letting the axe cool down."

Jenkins and Rogers Talk Pitching

August 24, 2009

Conventional baseball wisdom, if not logic, holds that pitching is seventy percent of the game. In the midst of a half-dozen tight divisional and wild card races in late August, it seems more like around eighty percent. So this weekend at the Best College Scholarship Sports Celebrity Golf Tournament, when we got the chance to hold an informal pitching summit with legendary right-handers Ferguson Jenkins and Steve Rogers, we were there with a beer.

We must preface what you are about to read with a gargantuan tip of the hat. Everyone born before 1970 should already know Hall of Famer Fergie Jenkins was a seven-time twenty game winner for the Cubs and Rangers, including six in a row starting in 1967, with a Cy Young Award in 1971. Almost as many should know Steve Rogers during the '70s and early '80s trailed only the likes of Steve Carlton and Tom Seaver as a dominant starter in the National League.

What few of us fully recall is what workhorses these guys were. By today's standards, their durability was supernatural. Rogers averaged about 250 innings over more than ten seasons. He pitched a remarkable 129 complete games. Jenkins tossed above 300 innings in five separate campaigns, with—no, this is not a typo—267 complete games in his career. In 1971 alone, he made it through a full nine innings an astounding 30 times. Not only do staffs no longer reach this plateau—entire divisions do not. When these two gentlemen, representing a total of 396 complete games, pontificated on strength and stamina, we listened.

The veteran righties tell us the pitch count has become king, to the detriment of the sport. Over the years, 100 pitches went from being an indicator to being the law, and the result has been the opposite of what was intended—a weakening rather than strengthening of arms. Fergie reminisced about getting fitted for a suit circa 1972. His tailor was flabbergasted by the difference of several inches between Fergie's right and left shoulders and wondered how he was going to marry a size 46 jacket to a size 52 arm.

The sartorial problem was a byproduct of not only conditioning but innings. In the trial-by-fire era of baseball, the Incredible Hulk side of Fergie's torso rose to the challenge. Rogers experienced a smaller but proportional benefit to his physique and balanced it with extra resistance training for his left side. The entire upper body was balanced with a marathon's worth of leg work each week, which helped propel the righties to the eighth inning and beyond literally hundreds of times.

By comparison, today's starters are expected roughly every six days to go five innings, or what Milt Pappas called "five and fly." Six innings, or what the veteran righties call an incomplete game, may qualify as a "quality start." Box scores are full of holds and lefty-lefty match-ups, and the game has suffered. Nine innings takes three-and-a-half hours. Still, hitting often dominates in late innings, Sabermetrics be darned. Teams carry as many as thirteen or fourteen pitchers at times, translating to fewer position players and fewer good offensive options at the end of a ballgame.

It took Jenkins and Rogers to remind us that back in the day a team typically carried nine pitchers in April and maybe a tenth in May. Jenkins was that tenth man when he broke in during the '65 campaign. As a reliever he almost never entered a game to face one batter and leave. In the era that spawned Rollie Fingers, Goose Gossage, Lee Smith and Bruce Sutter, a six-out save was nothing unusual.

The consensus at the summit was that the pitch count and low expectations were a self-fulfilling prophesy and a leading cause of pitchers failing to reach their potential. A non-pitcher in the group suggested the Roger Bannister model. Back in 1954, some observers thought a sub-four minute mile exceeded human capacity. For years, milers approached the four-minute mark then faded. When the young, slender Oxford grad finally proved otherwise by crossing the finish line six tenths of a second below four flat, he was filmed collapsing from exhaustion for newsreels the world over. But in the ensuing months, several runners broke four minutes with little drama.

Fortunately for the veteran righties, a savior has come to the game in the form of their peer, Hall of Famer Nolan Ryan. As president of the Texas Rangers, Ryan has his staff conditioning their legs old school and pitching till it hurts, or beyond. The Rangers have all but thrown out the pitch count, choosing to let opposing hitters inform them—via their lumber—when the pitchers are running out of gas.

With well over 5,000 strikeouts, including over 1,000 during his forties, that same approach worked for Ryan. And with the Texas staff producing remarkable seasons from a group of largely unknown hurlers while the team battles the Red Sox for the wild card, old school seems to be staging a comeback.

"Always ready to throw nine."

A Rain Delay to Remember

August 31, 2009

Forty years ago, half a million people at Woodstock had fun in the rain. Saturday night at Citizens Bank Park, we did too. Around six o'clock, a monsoon swept through Philadelphia, and we ducked into the Braves clubhouse to kill some time. About a third of the active roster was at one end of the room huddled around the flat screen watching a reel of outtakes and bloopers from the movie *Anchorman*. When we saw Steve "Brick" Carell's mock-promo spot—*When there's weather, I cover the weather—*

We knew we had come to the right place.

On the outskirts of the film festival was reliever Peter Moylan. A native of Australia, Moylan has posted a 3.18 ERA in 72 games so far this year. Two seasons ago, the Aussie appeared in 80 games and posted an ERA of 1.80. To paraphrase Crocodile Dundee, now that's an earned run average. But Moylan's most outstanding feature is his array of tattoos. What started as an experiment on one arm became body armor from neck to waist.

Running into Chipper Jones was somewhat of a reunion. Jones, who is steadfastly closing in on the dual plateaus of 3,000 hits and 500 homeruns, is also a top bow and gun enthusiast. He recently purchased several hundred acres of land in both Oklahoma and south Texas for sport and preservation. A couple of years ago, one of us ran into Chipper at the induction ceremonies in Indianapolis for the Archery Hall of Fame.

Being inducted that year, posthumously, was Dave Staples, founder of the Hall and the catalyst behind the inclusion of archery as an Olympic sport in 1972. He was also someone one of us called Dad. At the inductions, Chipper paid his respects. Now during the rain delay, we presented the future Baseball Hall of Fame third baseman with a program from the 2007 Archery HOF induction, and for one brief moment awe did a turnaround.

This Kodak moment was strangely interrupted by the sound of a voice from out of nowhere: "Billy! Billy, where are you, man?" Problem was, the voice had no clear origin. It took Adam Liberman to explain that it emanated from former Braves catcher and current bullpen coach Eddie Perez. Perez, in addition to being a ten-year big league veteran, is also an accomplished ventriloquist. He practices his art on unsuspecting clubhouse visitors at odd times, like during rain delays.

Liberman should know things like this. He's Senior Coordinator, the number two guy in the Braves media relations office. After graduating from Ohio University, Liberman became director of communications for the Akron Racers of the Women's Pro Softball League. Seeking the bigtime, he applied for a job as a publicity intern with the Atlanta Braves just before the 2000 season. Normally the position, which opened up immediately following the 1999 season, would have long since been filled. But in January 2000, the Braves media relations department had their hands full with relief pitcher John Rocker's provocative comments in a now infamous *Sports Illustrated* interview. Liberman points out the irony of Rocker's rant against an array of ethnicities ultimately allowing the hiring of a Jewish guy who would go on to help run the department.

That same year, at the All-Star game at Turner Field in Atlanta, Adam Liberman would find himself in the Braves dugout flanked by Frank Robinson on one side and Reggie Jackson on the other. Stultified by the notion of being surrounded by over 1,100 homeruns, Liberman told himself to take a deep breath and remember he had a job to do. Within a few years he had exhaled, and when during a trip to Philadelphia former manager Jim Fregosi made a crack about Liberman's goatee being somewhat effeminate, the rising PR star took matters into his own hands. Using Photoshop like an old pro, he drew a believable goatee onto a headshot of Fregosi.

The photo made the rounds in the two clubhouses and got a barrel of laughs. And like many other successful gags, the doctored photo kept making the rounds. When in 2007 the Phillies put together a tribute to fallen coach John Vukovich, a publicity intern found the shot on a hard drive, and Fregosi's goatee photo wound up on the back of the 8x10 souvenir given to fans. If anyone out there has one of the forty thousand copies handed out that night, hold on to it. It may be a collector's item.

As the rain lightened up, the Braves starter, Derek Lowe, walked by hurriedly. We asked our master of ceremonies if we should try to get a quote or two from Lowe, and we were told not to bother right now. Lowe has a touch of ADD, and before a start it tends to peak. We took Liberman's word for it. He has helped set a great tone for the Braves organization, and as both a PR director and a raconteur, the former women's softball staffer is in a league of his own.

"Fregosi without the goatee."

Hanson Fills Big Shoes for the Braves

September 7, 2009

When the Atlanta Braves released Tom Glavine on June 3, they closed the door not only on 305 career wins but on an entire era. During nearly two decades where baseball was dominated by labor actions, luxury boxes, homeruns, and steroids, the Braves won division title after title primarily on starting pitching. The triumvirate of Maddux, Glavine, and Smoltz stood up to any staff comparison pulled from the pages of history.

Enter Thomas J Hanson. No one ever compared Hanson directly to Glavine, first names aside. For starters, Hanson is a righty. But the call-up of Hanson from Gwinnett the same week was not lost on many people who followed the Braves. There was suddenly a lot of weight on the shoulders of a pitcher drafted in the 22nd round, 677th overall, in 2005.

On the other hand, the Braves know pitching. Since June 7, Tommy Hanson is 9-3 with and ERA of 3.07. Don't look now, but the lanky 6'3" prospect out of San Bernardino, California is creeping up on the Phillies' J.A. Happ for NL Rookie of the Year honors. While the J in J.A. Happ stands for James, Hanson tells us the J in his name doesn't stand for anything in particular. But it might as well stand for June or July. He was NL Rookie of the Month for June and kept right on blazing into the summer, beating both the Yankees and Red Sox while they were focused on beating each other.

It didn't begin so smoothly. In his Major League debut against the Brewers, Hanson was touched up for six earned runs and three homeruns, two of them by Ryan Braun. The shelling of *Baseball America's* number four prospect is preserved for posterity on YouTube but fell off Tommy Hanson's radar in about a day.

Spend an hour or two with Hanson and you'll get a feel for why. He looks and carries himself like a younger version of actor-director Ron Howard. There is an apple pie quality that shines through his smile and body language. His birthplace is Tulsa, Oklahoma, but Hanson spent only the first couple of years there while his dad finished Bible college. By the time Tommy could comprehend reruns of *Happy Days*, his family was back in California.

Dad was an ironworker up and out of the house by dawn. Mom was a homemaker and later an administrator with Costco. She was raised by a widower struggling with five kids on a small salary, so higher education at the time was not an option. Together, Thomas and Cynthia raised four kids of their own and made it so money wasn't a barrier.

The second of those kids, Thomas J., clearly had a knack for baseball. Dad didn't know the game all that well but learned it and worked with his prodigy son on the front lawn. When things got more serious, Dad paid for private lessons for Tommy with local coaches and, when possible, with former minor leaguers. Mom, meanwhile, kept it light by taking the kids up to Lake Arrowhead two or three times a month. There, they fed the ducks McDonald's French fries and stole a couple for themselves.

When Tommy was around 12, his parents separated. While this seems to be almost the norm for the generation now entering the American workforce, the shattering of your biological family can only happen once. According to Tommy Hanson, however, it was not especially traumatic for him. He still had a close relationship to both his mother and father, and they were both still accessible.

As it turns out, close families don't fade away, they just reorganize. Tommy is close as ever to his mom. His dad, stepmom, and two younger sisters have relocated to Kennesaw, Georgia to be nearer to Tommy. For no reason other than good fortune, they were all in attendance during the spring of 2008 when Tommy threw a no-hitter for the double-A Mississippi Braves. In the first inning, Hanson issued two walks and beaned a batter to load the bases with one out. Talk about unshakeable.

At barely 23 years of age, Tommy Hanson of the Atlanta Braves alternates between a fastball around 96 MPH and a curveball that hooks in on lefties like an air show dive bomber. He is all business on the mound and can turn it on whenever he has to, which as the Braves fight desperately for a wild card spot will be often this month. Still, Hanson is so unassuming in person, when he is told during our interview that manager Bobby Cox needs to speak to the team at 4:45, we feel personally responsible for making sure the young pitcher is there on time.

Though Tommy Hanson's aura is disarming, it won't make his stuff any more hittable. If anything, it may be one more advantage for the rising righty.

"Tommy's the tall one."

JETER'S NEXT HURDLE

September 14, 2009

Now that Derek Jeter has gotten over the hump and passed Lou Gehrig as the all-time Yankees leader in hits, there is another statistical hurdle immediately before the prolific shortstop. Of course, both Jeter and the spirit of Gehrig will tell you in a heartbeat no individual player is as important as the team, and nothing the team does is as important as winning. But this next benchmark is, at least, a team record.

If sometime between tonight and October 4 Derek Jeter can muster three longballs, the 2009 New York Yankees will become the first team ever to have eight players with 20 or more homeruns for the season.

For many years, those baseball fans born in the '50s and '60s kept a list in our heads of similar feats. The list needed updating only occasionally. There were two teams with one player hitting 60 or more dingers—the '27 Yankees with Ruth's 60, and the '61 Yankees with Maris's 61, asterisks be darned.

That same '61 Yankees team, of course, had the only pair to hit 50 or more—Mantle and Maris. Less well known is that the same team had six players with 20 or more homeruns—the M&M Boys, plus Yogi Berra, Elston Howard, platoon catcher Johnny Blanchard, and first baseman Bill Skowron.

Moving down the line, the 1973 Atlanta Braves had the only trio to hit 40 or more—Hank Aaron, Darrell Evans, and the second baseman having a career year and then some, future manager Davey Johnson. A few years later, in 1977, the Los Angeles Dodgers set the record for the

30-homerun threshold with four players: Steve Garvey, Ron Cey, Reggie Smith, and Dusty Baker. And that was basically the comfortable, secure statistical world the Apollo 11-Woodstock-Watergate-OPEC Oil Crisis generation lived in for quite some time.

Until that world was rocked. Maybe it was the anabolic steroids. Maybe it was the intense resistance training initiated by Tony La Russa. Maybe it was the smaller strike zone, the new hitters' parks, expansion, livelier balls, and better engineered lumber. Maybe it was all of the above. Nonetheless, we of the *Star Trek* generation found ourselves living in a strange universe where Brady Anderson could spank 50 pitches over the Gillette sign.

The team homerun plateau records began to fall to the point where, frankly, we lost track. McGwire and Bonds established a new 70-plus category. The one-team, one-man 60-homerun record more or less remained, but with Sammy Sosa by himself reaching it in three of four seasons, it suddenly seemed like no big whoop. As for the smaller plateaus, suffice it to say we developed a migraine Saturday night cruising the internet into the wee hours trying to make some sense of it all.

Led by Ken Griffey Jr. and Jay Buhner, the 1997 Seattle Mariners had six players socking 20 or more round-trippers, with A-Rod and his 23 dingers helping to bring up the rear. The Baltimore Orioles of the same era deserve an honorable mention, not only for flirting with six 20-homerun players in 1998 but for fielding 10 (yes, 10!) players with 10 or more goners. As an Orioles platoon player that year, Harold Baines had 9. The Birds did it again in 2000. As the sad story goes, they finished fourth in the AL East both seasons.

But the 20-homerun record appears to have been shattered by the Texas Rangers of 2005, around the very time when juicing started to lose some of its juice. The Mark Teixeira-led Rangers had lost A-Rod the season before but filled his spot in the lineup with the Yankees' Alfonso Soriano, one of seven players to hit at least 20 homeruns for Buck Showalter in '05. This was a team so thoroughly and uniformly dinger-prone that Gary Matthews Jr. and Richard Hidalgo hit 17 and 16 respectively while both playing far short of 162 games.

Now here come the 2009 Yankees, chock full of walk-offs and postgame pies and so well rounded that only Mark Teixeira has a shot at 40. Alex Rodriguez—Kate Hudson rooting section and all—is sitting in the middle of the pack with 25. Superstars like Johnny Damon and Jeter are contact hitters whose line drives occasionally get up, while switch-hitters like Jorge Posada and Nick Swisher help confound opposing pitchers. Rounded out by second baseman Robinson Cano and DH Godzilla Matsui, only the centerfield position is more about speed than pop.

In the end, none of this may be important except as a way for sportswriters to avoid paying their quarterly taxes another couple of days. But lies, damn lies, and statistics aside, these numbers may actually mean something come October. The 2009 Yankees are one of the most balanced offensive teams in the history of the game. There is no one to pitch around unless as a pitcher you prefer to get burned by one player rather than another. This team feat was achieved—albeit in a new stadium kind to the longball—in a year without expansion and with controlled substances more or less in the rear view mirror. And that's a squad worthy of a Jeter or a Gehrig as captain.

"On his toes."

THE WRIGHT STUFF

September 21, 2009

The last time we had the pleasure of sitting down with David Wright for a good long talk was right after the 2006 baseball season. The Mets had won the NL East, beaten the Dodgers, and then lost a seven game thriller to the eventual World Series Champion St. Louis Cardinals. Back then, Wright exhibited a combination of disappointment and resolve after coming within an inning of going to the World Series but was upbeat and personable.

With almost another three complete Major League campaigns behind him, Wright has been seasoned by disappointments and frustrations that make the 2006 saga seem like a fairytale. The 2007 Mets collapse has entered the pantheon of baseball skids (move over '64 Phillies), and 2008 was a painful if less dramatic encore. The Mets this season were more injury plagued than the set of a Vin Diesel movie, and Wright's cranial collision with a Matt Cain fastball on August 15 left the New York metropolitan region holding its collective breath.

Happily, Wright is a hundred percent, and never once—then or now—has there ever been an ounce of quit in the talented third baseman. Still, as we unwind late at night in the empty back room of a hotel restaurant in Philadelphia, we have an unspoken agreement not to talk much baseball.

The ostensible reason we're here says a lot about David Wright. He was gracious enough in contributing his childhood story to our 2007 book project, *Before the Glory*. A spinoff of that effort is to raise money for the

BEST College Scholarship fund by getting players to sign copies of the book for charitable auction. No one in or out of baseball is faster to cooperate with such selfless endeavors than number 5 of the New York Mets.

In 2005, Wright seemingly had the world on a string. In his first full season as a Met, he hit for power and average, produced in clutch situations, and proved he was here to stay. Like Mantle, Gifford, Namath, Pepitone, and Clyde Frazier before him, David Wright was a good looking young guy with superstar qualities dropped into the media and nightlife capital of the world. Setting a trend all his own, he used that perch to establish the David Wright Foundation, becoming one of the youngest ballplayers ever to take the full plunge into a life of giving back.

Wright focuses on fighting children's diseases, especially multiple sclerosis. His off-seasons are packed with visits to hospitals and fundraisers and peak with the late fall banquet, "Do the Wright Thing." This gala in the Times Square area raises hundreds of thousands of dollars and in its fifth year has taken on that special aura of the place to be, much like Joe Torre's "Safe at Home" event. Wright's team includes superagent Seth Levinson of ACES, liaison and former Met Keith Miller, and ACES support person Anna. Like their unique star player, they are less interested in building bankrolls than role models.

That's the way Wright prefers to use the cachet of his stats, stature and smile. He told us that right about when he started to click in New York, he was amazed at what a few words or gestures from a marquee player could do to help people and decided to bottle it while he could.

But the wear and tear of a tough season is palpable. Wright talks about those portions of the off-season when he will not be running the bases for charities but relaxing on a beach in Barbados or Costa Rica. Hard as it is to believe, he tells us pretty much all he does near the equator during those days is sit on the beach and swirl his toes in the sand. We mention there are awe inspiring active volcanoes in Costa Rica, but Wright admits he is so spent by December the lava will have to come to him.

The baseball part of our chat comes not from Wright himself but from surging Padres closer and former teammate of David Wright's, Heath Bell. Bell recalls Wright being the one guy in the clubhouse who was "lights on, 24/7." Wright was up for every at-bat, every ground ball, every reporter, and every opportunity to contribute right up until the moment he landed on the shores of Barbados.

The night we signed books for charity was September 11, an uneasy anniversary to begin with, and one on which in 2009 Wright and the Mets have been silenced 4-2 at Citizens Bank Park by Cole Hamels and the Phillies. The trash talk over the winter was something David Wright stayed out of as he does now after a thrashing. Instead, the following afternoon, Wright goes back to the ballpark and bangs two homeruns and six RBI against the World Champs. This is no hype. This is the real David Wright.

"Doing it Wright."

How the Yankees Won the West

September 28, 2009

Tuesday night's Yankee game against the Los Angeles Angels was a chance to relive childhood memories. Here was a West Coast game on a school night broadcast on non-subscription TV during a pennant race. As the game pushed past 1 AM EST, there was the fear that a parent was going to barge in and turn off the set, until you realized that this time around you *were* the parent.

Good thing, too. This game was impossible to turn off. It was critical to the race, a microcosm of the Yankees' season, and about as good a preview of the postseason as a baseball junkie could ask for.

For the Yankees, going to Anaheim has been like going to Disneyland with no money. You wish you had never made the trip. The Bombers hadn't won a series in Angels Stadium since 2004, were eliminated there in the 2005 League Divisional Series, and carried in an abysmal record of 4 and 14 going back to 2006. But this time was different. This is 2009. A-Rod, Hideki Matsui, and Jorge Posada each homered to give the Yanks a 5-0 lead.

It didn't last. Human run-scoring machine Chone Figgins hit a solo homerun, as rare as a frown from Mickey Mouse. Two hits and a walk chased newcomer Chad Gaudin one out away from his second Yankee win. Alfredo Acevas stopped the bleeding but allowed some of his own with a smattering of singles in the sixth inning, which helped trigger the early arrival of set-up man supreme Phil Hughes.

When we spoke with Hughes recently, he was keenly aware of his position in Yankees history so early in his career. He is to Mariano Rivera in 2009 what Rivera was to John Wetteland in 1996. In 1995, Rivera had been a spot starter for the surging Mattingly-led Yankees and earned his relief stripes in the playoffs against the Seattle Mariners. In '96, new manager Joe Torre inserted Rivera into the set-up slot, and the Yankees' season reduced to the challenge of taking a one-run lead into the seventh inning.

Phil Hughes has been lights out in much the same way this year, posting an ERA of a bit over 1.00 in 41 relief appearances. No one is more surprised than Hughes himself that this was his path back to the show. When we talked in April during his assignment with Scranton/Wilkes-Barre, he was focused entirely on throwing strikes and turning in quality starts. Over the summer, Hughes told us in spite of the curveball he was thrown by Manager Joe Girardi upon returning to the Bronx (guess who caught Rivera and Wetteland back in '96), landing in this pivotal role was about the best thing that's ever happened to him.

The eighth inning of Tuesday night's game, however, was not the best thing that ever happened to Phil Hughes. An error by Robinson Cano and then an error by Jorge Posada trying to throw out Howie Kendrick stealing second set up the run that tied the game 5-5. For Hughes, the run was unearned. For Posada, the throwing error was excusable, because a few minutes earlier he had been hit by a back-swing on his surgically repaired right shoulder. But for the Yankees as a whole, the odds of being sent home again penniless from Disneyland loomed large. And then six-foot-five Philip Hughes manned up and blew away Vlad Guerrero and Torii Hunter on nasty fastballs to send the ride into the ninth.

The ninth inning turned out to be the Yankees' most impressive of the season and justified bleary eyes the next morning as the kids' lunches were packed. Gardner got on with a hard single to right and then proceeded to take his lead. This was a lead—while being held on by pitcher Matt Palmer, mind you—so ridiculously long you thought the runner had depth perception problems or perhaps had forgotten he was not the back end of a double steal.

On chutzpah and speed, Gardner stole second, and moments later Derek Jeter walked. Johnny Damon has been more of a power guy this year than a conventional two-slot hitter, but on this night he lay down a perfect bunt to move over Jeter and Gardner. When Alex Rodriguez came to the plate, it didn't feel like 2004 or any other season between then and now. A-Rod has tied a game or produced a go-ahead run with an RBI 47 times this season. Yes, it's just the regular season, but Rodriquez lined a sac-fly to left-center like a fungo in an instructional video and sent Garner home in a go-ahead blur.

In the ninth, Mo did in 2009 what Wetteland did in 1996 and what Rivera himself has done well over 500 times since. The Yankees proved they could beat arguably their toughest American League rival not simply with power but with fundamental small-ball. Without even a legitimate number five starter, they turned a corner in the middle of the night. The only thing missing was a walk-off homerun.

"42 means no Mo runs."

DON'T COUNT LIDGE OUT

October 5, 2009

When Charlie Manuel called Brad Lidge from the bullpen last Wednesday night to get the final out against the Houston Astros to clinch the National League East title for the third straight season, most onlookers tipped their cap to the manager for a classy sentimental gesture. It wasn't entirely sentimental.

Neither was putting in Lidge Saturday night against the Marlins in the ninth inning for a three-up-three-down outing. Running out as a team after clinching Wednesday night to spray champagne on the Harry Kalas sign in leftfield—now *that* was sentimental.

But Charlie Manuel is not the leader of a spiritual encounter group or a 12-step program. He is a Major League manager trying to do something extremely rare in baseball—win back-to-back World Series Championships. Virtually every lineup move Manuel made over the past week figured somehow into that plan. With Jamie Moyer and Chan Ho Park down for the count, the final days before the League Division Series became a combination fact-finding mission and exploratory surgery.

Surgery is a word that gets Brad Lidge talking if he has a few moments. An articulate guy to begin with, he sometimes sounds as if he spends his off-seasons in med school. During the period from 1998 through early 2003—a span that includes essentially Lidge's entire minor league career, the pitcher arguably experienced enough physical problems and surgeries to receive credit for at least a semester or two.

In Class A Quad Cities, as a hard throwing starter with a decent curveball, the back of Lidge's elbow hurt and was chronically swollen. The team shut him down for the season. The thinking was Lidge had started on a once-a-week basis in Notre Dame and was now suddenly subjected to throwing every fifth day. The six-hour workouts in college had been a shock coming out of high school, and the cumulative effect of everything was taking its toll.

However, early in the next season at Kissimmee, Florida, essentially the same thing happened. The following season, 2000, also at Kissimmee, was turning into déjà vu all over again when pitching coach Dewey Robinson stepped in. Robinson shut down Lidge for two months, but not simply to heal. The curveball was stricken from Lidge's repertoire. It turned out the hook was creating excessive stress on Lidge's elbow due to the nearness of the hand to the head in the throwing motion. To Dewey Robinson's credit, when Lidge reemerged later that season his new slider provided a pain free alternative to the curve and got batters out efficiently.

As the story is supposed to go, the pitcher moves up quickly and sails into his role as a dominant Major League closer. But instead, a few starts back into his new lease on baseball life, a line drive is hit back to the box. Lidge puts up his right hand, and his ulna is broken in two. Enter a four-inch steel plate into Lidge's right wrist.

The medical saga, at this point, is just beginning, and the insufficient length of our story may be supplemented by a read through *Gray's Anatomy*. The new arm angle caused shoulder problems in 2001 to the point where Lidge couldn't pull the covers over his head at night. Next step: Surgery for rotator cuff and labrum repairs. Then Lidge got a cup of coffee after only about 100 actual innings in the minors and felt severe pain in his right knee. More surgery, this time to repair the meniscus and a hole in his cartilage.

It wasn't until the 2003 season with the Houston Astros that Brad Lidge was a) healthy, and b) officially a closer. He then began a five-year run of success at the Major League level. Wrist, elbow, shoulder and knee—an aggregate miracle of modern science—all worked perfectly together and ultimately helped to produce the 2008 season, perhaps the best in the storied history of relief pitching.

When Lidge tells us he feels okay, we believe him. He is one of the most sincere gentlemen you will ever find, in or out of baseball. The sincerity includes an admission that his game is now more about pitch selection than cutting loose and that his problems of late are more a performance issue than one of velocity. "The ship has always righted itself," he says. "I know it will again."

There is no room for sentiment in the postseason. Lidge and his manager are competitors and realists, and the pitcher will go out to the rubber in any situation he can help the team. One odd benefit of Lidge's early years of physical turmoil, however, is the mental discipline it taught him. His next trip to the mound will be a challenge, but he is psyched up, not psyched out.

"The Lidges and a close friend."

JIM KAAT'S MANY LIVES

October 12, 2009

It wasn't hard this weekend to find folks to talk playoff baseball, especially with the down time provided by Saturday's snow-out of the Phillies and Rockies in Denver. But we had the privilege of chewing the fat with legendary pitcher Jim Kaat. A beloved, Emmy Award-winning broadcaster as well, Kitty Kaat is obviously highly qualified to provide insight. Factor in that at various times he played for four of the eight teams in this year's postseason—the Twins, Phillies, Yankees, and Cardinals—and there may be no one better suited.

But when you're speaking to a man who pitched in 25 seasons touching four decades, won 283 decisions, and took home 16 Gold Gloves, there is a lot more to cover than insights from the past few days. Kaat is known for having nine lives, and from the looks of his still rock solid 6'4" frame, at age 70 he may only be on life number five or six.

The last member of the original Washington Senators to appear in a big league game, Kaat was an original Minnesota Twin with an easy lefty motion that belied his hard fastball and nasty screwball. When Kaat and the Twins made it to the World Series in 1965, they were a long shot against Sandy Koufax, Don Drysdale, and the Los Angeles Dodgers, who two seasons before had blanked the Yankees four games to none.

Having played his first seven seasons in the American League and having limited access to NBC's *Game of the Week* due to his own career, Kaat had never seen more than a snippet of Koufax. So the day before the series when the Twins' top lefty walked by the Dodgers' top lefty, who was warming up, Jim Kaat heard a powerful woosh of air that turned his head. It was a nearly supersonic Koufax fastball, powered by a motion that was so complete and a release so over the top it could have been filmed and shown in physiology class.

It was cold in Minneapolis in October. Koufax called over to the unassuming Kaat and asked if they actually played in weather like this. "All the time," Kaat told him. Kaat thought the climate might be the only way the Twins could take Koufax and the Dodgers. But then someone with even better stuff than Koufax intervened—God.

October 6, 1965 happened to be Yom Kippur, so while Koufax observed the Jewish holiday, Don Drysdale started Game 1 for the Dodgers against the Twins' righty ace, Mudcat Grant. The Twinkies' powerful lineup quickly scored six runs, powered by homeruns from shortstop Zoilo Versalles and first baseman Don Mincher. When with two outs in the bottom of the third inning Dodger manager Walter Alston walked out to the mound to take the ball from Drysdale, the tall right-hander said, "I bet you wish I was Jewish."

Kaat and his teammates got some more help from above in Game 2 when an error and a couple of soft singles in the sixth inning helped chase Sandy Koufax. Not only did Kaat pitch a complete game that day for the Twins and allow only one run, but late in the game he added a single up the middle with the bases loaded off reliever Ron Perranoski to make it 5-1 Twins. Of course, Kaat was perfectly capable of helping himself. That year he not only won 18 games and a Gold Glove but hit .247 with 9 RBI.

In another life, Kaat fractured the navicular bone in his left wrist and was traded late in the 1973 season to the White Sox when the Twins organization believed his career was winding down. In Chicago, however, Kaat rejoined former Minnesota pitching coach and four-time 20-game winner Johnny Sain. Sain and Kaat worked on the quick pitch, which Kaat describes as something like a throw to home plate after fielding a ground ball with the bases loaded. The no-windup approach caught a lot of hitters off guard, made Kaat a 20-game winner again in both '74 and '75, and—perhaps best of all—kept ballgames to about two hours.

In his current life, Jim Kaat the baseball analyst picks class act Derek Jeter and the Yankees to win it all but has been privately rooting for the Twins and Phillies. Kaat still sees the old Twins in the great fundamental ball played by today's Minnesota club. As for the Phils, Kaat is friends with Charlie Manuel dating back to their playing days in Minnesota.

But perhaps the most important factor in Jim Kaat's present life reveals itself when we bring to dinner a friend named Russ Barnett. Barnett was a fellow lefty pitcher when Kaat started out in 1957 in Class D ball summer league in the booming metropolis of Superior, Nebraska, population roughly 2,000. Fifty-two years later, Kaat not only remembered Barnett but reeled off a story about how there were two Barnett pitchers on the team (the other actually spelled "Barnette") and how one of them reported to the wrong town. What makes Jim Kaat a really special human being is not how many lives he's lived but the importance he's always placed on other lives.

"Kaat, Russ, and Rich."

BRAVES' GREG NORTON NO STRANGER TO ADVERSITY

October 16, 2009

There may be no role in baseball more difficult than pinch hitter. Hitting a round ball with a round bat squarely is vexing as it is. As the pitcher goes into his motion, a proficient batter's outside world begins to shut down, leaving only a 60-foot, 6-inch long cylinder. If he is to be successful, crowd noise, scoreboard images, and what a pop out will do to his average fall off the face of the Earth.

For a pinch hitter, the situation is even more severe. His first turn at the plate isn't a warm-up. It isn't a chance to check out the pitcher's stuff and think about driving a pitch in the next at-bat, because there is no next at-bat.

For a good number of years, Greg Norton of the White Sox, Rockies, Tigers, Rays, Mariners, and most recently the Atlanta Braves has been one of the premier pinch hitters in Major League Baseball. Among current players, his lifetime 13 pinch hit homeruns are second only to Matt Stairs. Norton is tied for eleventh all-time on that same list.

Playing for the Braves in 2008, Norton hit .316 in 74 pinch hitting plate appearances and compiled a Barry Bonds-like .473 on-base percentage. One might think Greg Norton's success as a pinch hitter is a gift life bestowed on him. Nothing could be further from the truth.

Norton grew up in the scenic Montclair district of Oakland, California in the 1980s. Like a lot of athletically talented kids, he skipped T-ball and played Little League with the older kids. By his early teens, Norton learned that the best competition was offered by the racially mixed areas of downtown Oakland. So his father, Jerry, who once played in the Pirates organization and trained in jungle warfare during the Vietnam era, drove Greg to where the action was every game he could.

Life was good for Greg Norton. His older brother, Tim, a journeyman college football quarterback, had experienced more of his parents' early economic struggle than Greg. By the time Greg came of age, his father was a successful CPA and his mother owned and operated two well regarded day schools. The Nortons lived in an attractive four-story house up on a hill. Greg was a good natured kid with a mischievous side and was even a little spoiled. A brush fire he set in the rear yard resulted in the taking away of his BMX bike, but his sports life remained intact.

On the morning of Saturday, May 6, 1989, Greg Norton arose early to take the SAT. He felt a little uneasy and self-conscious, but not so much because of the exam. He would probably be playing ball in a couple of years at a Division I college, and a combined math and verbal score of 1000 or so would be more than enough to open any door. Strangely, a different door—the one to the front of the house—happened to be open slightly, and he gently closed it.

He had come in past curfew from a date the night before and probably disturbed his parents by punching in the alarm code on the keypad by the garage. Before going out, he had argued briefly with his mother about a shirt she declined to iron for him, and now in the morning he owed it to his folks to let them sleep. Still, he had a strange feeling he needed to climb the stairs to their bedroom on the fourth floor.

When he got there and looked into the bedroom there was no sound, and something wasn't quite right. When he checked on his mom, she was motionless. Greg looked for his dad, but he was nowhere to be found.

Life changed drastically for Greg Norton on that day. By the afternoon the police had interrogated him. By early evening he was informed that his mother had been murdered. By nightfall he had moved in with his friend's parents. By 1 AM the police had called to say they were charging his father with the crime.

How Greg Norton resumed his high school baseball career, bounced from college to college, reconnected with his brother, and finally landed in the big leagues is worthy of a book, and at least one is in the pipeline. However, a single salient detail that sticks in our heads after talking with Norton is how during those make-or-break years when he became distracted and overwhelmed, he would just get in the car, put on some music, and drive for hours.

For reasons no one has completely figured out, pinch hitter extraordinaire Greg Norton struggled at the plate this year, hovering around a buck-fifty and feeling he disappointed a team that fought till the end for a wild card spot. But wherever he lands next season, Greg Norton knows his fourteen-year Major League career is a small miracle and his solid marriage and two wonderful kids a much larger one. And for those who look at the numbers and say this is the roughest year of Greg Norton's life, it is not. Not even close.

"Norton and Rich get the details right."

Phillies Win More Than a Game

October 19, 2009

Everyone who follows baseball—or who doesn't—has heard the "one game at a time" cliché in one form or another. Sunday, we heard every conceivable form, until the idea, if not the precise words, became a mantra. From Charlie Manuel's standard pregame comments to Joe Torre's postgame aphorism ("They only beat us once"), to a dozen or more players' comments in the clubhouse, we virtually OD'ed on the game-at-a-time truism.

One problem, though—the truism isn't exactly true. While the Phillies didn't win two games in their 11-0 trouncing of the Dodgers Sunday night, they won more than a game. Maybe one-and-a-quarter. Maybe one-and-a-third. Hard as it is to quantify, the Phillies won more than a game.

For starters, the Phillies eliminated the Hiroki Kuroda bugaboo. The righty had been virtually unhittable for the Phils during the regular season. Now, however, the Kuroda option is largely off the table for the Dodgers. After that drubbing, Torre will be hesitant to go to Kuroda again even in a relief situation. Kuroda's location was less than outstanding, and his movement was average. Charlie Manuel's pregame statements about working the count turned out prophetic. Bottom line, the next time Kuroda's name pops into Joe Torre's mind, he will flashback to Jayson Werth's jaw-dropping monster shot to Ashburn Alley at Citzens Bank Park.

Next, the Dodgers do not want to see Cliff Lee again this series. Ever, if possible. Unfortunately for the Dodgers, the only control they have over that is to lose in five games. The prospect of facing Lee in a Game 6 or 7 casts a shadow over Games 4 and 5. Cliff Lee not only faced two over the minimum number of batters through eight innings, he was nearly unhittable. The 114 pitches and 76 for strikes tell only a narrow statistical side of the story. Lee's strikeout of Rafael Furcal in the sixth inning comes to mind. Furcal missed the lefty's looping, Andy Pettitte-like curveball by about two feet and fell down like Reggie Jackson without the power stroke.

The Phillies, meanwhile, neutralized the Dodgers' slight bullpen advantage dating back to Game 2 in Los Angeles. The Dodgers' use of four hurlers out of the pen was highlighted by a three-and-a-third inning stint by starter Chad Billingsley, who is now that much less of an option to replace Kuroda in the rotation or even to throw long relief in Philadelphia. The Phils bullpen, meanwhile, other than a one-two-three ninth by another Chad (Durbin), had the night off. From Eyre to Happ to Madson to Lidge, their arms are loaded and ready.

After a rocky time on the West Coast, Chase Utley redeemed himself in the field several times. The monkey was clearly off his back as of the fifth inning, when he fielded a James Loney ground ball and threw accurately to Jimmy Rollins covering second base. There was a loud ironic cheer from the faithful at Citizens Bank, but that comes with the territory in the City of Brotherly Love. And it cuts two ways. After singling his first two times up, in his final at-bat Manny Ramirez was subjected to a booming chorus of "You did steroids!" It was a perfect example of Philly being Philly.

Last but not least, the Phillies appeared to be able to score runs at will. Now, just as the one-game-at-a-time truism is not quite true, neither is the one-at-bat-at-a-time mantra one hundred percent accurate. A batter can have a good at-bat without hitting as if his life depends on it. That is more or less what the Phillies did in the middle of innings of Game 3. They launched a couple of missiles in the early going and put a final nail in the coffin in the eighth inning on Shane Victorino's long homerun to right. There was no purpose in running up the score much more, especially given the low-40s temperature. No matter what the truisms say, this was not a Game 7.

Perhaps the oddest moment of Game 3 came when, after sending Cliff Lee to bat in the bottom of the eighth, Charlie Manuel pulled him for Chad Durbin in the top of the ninth. As Durbin walked to the mound, the reaction from about a thousand years of cumulative baseball experience in the press box was utter bemusement. The fact that Lee singled up the middle and scored on the Victorino homerun was beside the point. With an inning to go, a score of 11-0 isn't much more of a blowout than 8-0. But perhaps the outside chance that Lee might strain something in the frigid ninth inning prompted Manuel to push his second-thought button. And that's the bottom line in a pivotal Game 3. No matter what they say, it isn't exactly one game at a time.

"How sweet it is."

WORLD SERIES IN THE AIR FOR THE PHILS

October 20, 2009

There is a distinct World Series atmosphere building at 1 Citizens Bank Way. It grows with each game. It was palpable on the field before Game 4. There was *Meet the Press* host David Gregory chatting with Joe Torre for a good twenty minutes, each glad to be in the presence of the other and the entourage surrounding them both trying to catch a stray quote. There were Sandy Koufax in the stands with his bride and Tommy Lasorda upstairs in the press area on his way to somewhere important and gently nudging aside these two writers.

There was celebrated author William C. Rhoden in the Phillies clubhouse conferring with Ryan Howard on whether his team's ability to draw blood in the ninth inning was getting into the opponents' heads. There was Ford C. Frick Award winner Peter Gammons talking to just about everyone after the game in the media tent. There was even *CSI* cast member David Berman milling about.

These are postseason sights and sounds normally associated with New York or Los Angeles, and it's no coincidence that from hereon in, all road games for the Phils will be played in either of those two cities. But the Phillies have brought some of that center-of-the-universe mystique to the City of Brotherly Love, and they've done it with raw talent and clutch performances.

Regarding the game itself, as a journalist there are some games you are paid to report on, some you would do for free, and some you would gladly pay to cover. Game 4 was firmly in the last category. Sometime Monday night, the Phillies crossed over from a top notch defending World Series Champion to a team that may one day soon be mentioned in the same breath with the Yankees of the late '90s, the Oakland A's of the early '70s or even the Big Red Machine. And the best thing about that subtle transition Monday night was how hard the Dodgers made it.

No one in his right mind envisioned a second straight blowout, not even when Ryan Howard got a hold of a 3-1 fastball up and in from Randy Wolf in the bottom of the first inning for a two-run homerun. Wolf and the Dodgers bore down hard. The game had more subplots than an episode of *The Sopranos*.

Manny Ramirez is always good for at least one subplot. With only one extra-basehit in the series, Manny stepped to the plate in the fourth inning to loud chants of "You did steroids!" from the Philly faithful and responded with a rope down the left field line to break up Joe Blanton's early no-hitter. Between Manny's sluggish baserunning and the sharp carom off where the field level seats jut out, Ramirez didn't have his second extra-basehit, but the dreadlocked one got the last laugh when the fourth inning became a big one for the Dodgers.

Manny being Manny continued into the sixth inning when Shane Victorino lashed a ball of his own down the left field line. Victorino made it from home to third in what seemed like about eight seconds, still accelerating furiously as he rounded second base. Manny did his part by tracking down the ball with a nonchalance hardly befitting a team with its proverbial backside against the wall. But then Manny got one back a few batters later when he robbed Raul Ibanez of an RBI with a shoestring catch on a sinking line drive. The nail-biting had begun, as the Phils had pulled to within one run.

The eighth inning of this gem was played so much like a ninth inning that when it was over, we had to remind ourselves the real ninth inning hadn't yet begun. When Dodger reliever George Sherrill hit Shane Victorino with a pitch and then walked Chase Utley, there was practically no one in Citizens Bank Park who guessed Joe Torre would let Sherrill face Philadelphia's answer to Lou Gehrig, Ryan Howard. No one except Joe Torre, that is. The Jonathan Broxton-Ryan Howard battle of heavyweights was the one everyone had waited to see, but the fight was cancelled. Instead, Sherrill was left in to face Howard and struck him out. That's why they pay Joe Torre.

When Brad Lidge entered the game with one out and Rafael Furcal on first, the score still 4-3 Dodgers, the heavy metal boomed over the PA system. We couldn't identify the tune, but it might as well have been AC/DC's "Back in Black." Lidge is indeed back. You can see it in his fastball and slider and feel it in the way 46,000 fans expect success more than they dread failure. Lidge distracted himself by uncharacteristically throwing to first base three times. Furcal stole second anyway while Lidge struck out Matt Kemp. The exchange was a fair one, because Lidge's business is striking out the heart of the opponent's order, not holding runners on. A moment later, it was lights out for Andre Ethier as well.

The Broxton match-ups were undercard bouts for the bottom of the order. The Broxton-Stairs bout promised fireworks reminiscent of last October when Stairs's Game 4 homerun was the knockout blow. The déjà-vu was not to be realized. This time, it was a no-decision—a walk—which was fine for a Phillies club just looking for a baserunner.

When Jimmy Rollins turned on an inside fastball three batters later to drive home two and win this epic battle, the sounds pushed beyond the human aural threshold, shook the mezzanine, and even roused the normally sedate press box.

Though it may look, sound, and feel like the World Series, it is not quite yet. But it is time for New York and Los Angeles to start J-Rolling out the red carpet.

"Shane before the game."

The Phils are Scary Good

October 22, 2009

Just like movie or music critics, sportswriters are supposed to report objectively on what they see. Sometimes, however, a moment arrives when the product is just too good and you experience it like a fan. Like *The Godfather* or "Stairway to Heaven," the postseason Phillies Wednesday night reached a pinnacle where as a human being you had a duty at least for a moment to stand there and experience awe.

A clue that this moment was on its way was the emotion coming from the fans in the hour or so prior to Dallas Green throwing out the first ball. As packed and crazy as it had been outside the park and inside the corridors Sunday and Monday nights, on Wednesday this 46,000-plus put out a warlike vibe. Adrenaline vaporized amidst the fist-pumping faithful from Jenkintown, Lansdale, South Philly and Camden. There was just a little danger in the air, and you knew the crowd mentality was to go in for the kill. It was a warm night, so the press box windows were wide open, and there was no escaping the deafening noise.

In the early going, it seemed we were in for a hybrid of Games 3 and 4. There was a trading of blows that promised to become a nail-biter down the stretch. But no one can win a power war with the Philadelphia Phillies. Maybe the Yankees.

Andre Ethier's first inning right field blast off Cole Hamels announced the Dodgers were here to play. Jayson Werth's three-run homerun off a Vicente Padilla fastball out over the plate reminded the

Dodgers who they were dealing with. The second inning featured an exchange of leadoff homeruns by Dodgers first baseman James Loney and Phillies third baseman Pedro Feliz, neither one known especially for his power.

Orlando Hudson hit an impressive pinch hit homerun for the Dodgers down the left field line in the fifth inning, but that was where the trading of blows effectively ended. The clues were already there in the fourth inning when Werth and Raul Ibanez knocked out Padilla with a single and a double. What followed was something we can't recall ever seeing before in a postseason game. Righty reliever Ramon Troncoso hit Jimmy Rollins with a pitch. Troncoso was pulled for lefty reliever George Sherrill, who proceeded to plunk Shane Victorino with the bases loaded, making the score 6-2 Phillies.

Two key batters beaned consecutively by different pitchers in a tight spot. The consensus here was that this was no coincidence. The Dodgers knew what they were up against and experienced a twinge of desperation. They tried to back the Phillies off the plate, but the Phillies just dug in deeper. This was more than a symbolic stand. It was the turning point of the game.

From that point on, it was time for baseball fans—reporters or not—to appreciate fine art. Werth and Victorino were so zoned in we saw shades of Reggie Jackson in the '77 World Series. Victorino's first pitch sixth inning rope to the left field seats off Chad Billingsley was executed matter-of-factly as if from a hitman and fully utilized the strength in the centerfielder's compact Abrams tank of a body.

Werth's cannon shot in the seventh off a Hong-Chih Kuo 0-2 fastball sounded like a pine tree being snapped in two by Sasquatch and travelled from home plate to just left of Ashburn Alley in about the time it takes to scribble down the "o" in "outside corner." Victorino added a laser shot to right in the eighth inning that was the length of a fan's hand from another homerun and gave the impression that Shane was just getting warmed up.

Amidst the kudos to Chad Durbin for stabilizing the game and Park, Madson, and Lidge for nailing it down, knowledgeable voices around us were relegating Cole Hamels to long relief for the World Series. Perhaps. But while Hamels failed to live up to an '08 postseason virtually impossible to match, he wasn't as flat as the two solo homeruns might have indicated, and in lasting 4-1/3 innings put the Phillies in position to win. The grumbling over Hamels at this point is more than anything a reflection of how deep both the Phillies rotation and bullpen are. Everywhere Charlie Manuel looks there is a viable option.

It is even harder to maintain journalistic objectivity when surrounded in the clubhouse by a group of focused, gifted athletes approaching greatness, who are at the same time a bunch of big happy kids popping champagne bottles. It is just as hard not to root for a humble guy like Brad Lidge, who following Game 4 quipped, "Glad you were here for my first win of the year. I didn't expect it to be in October." But no one can be a clinician 24/7. Sometimes, you just have to appreciate how special something is.

"Werth every penny."

YANKEES VETERAN CORE SHOWS HOW IT'S DONE

November 1, 2009

There was no celebration in the Yankees clubhouse following Game 3 of the World Series—nothing even close to it. The mood was subdued and businesslike, with a few smiles breaking through now and again. As a team, the Yankees understood that they still had a long road ahead to make the promise of number 27 on their manager's back a reality.

After the team's 8-5 victory over the Phillies, the captain, Derek Jeter, set the tone in front of his locker. He noted the Yankees have experienced so many rain delays this season that the hour-and-twenty-minute hesitation on this Halloween night didn't spook them.

A moment later, Jeter grinned as he told reporters he almost lapped Andy Pettitte on the base path while running hard on Johnny Damon's fifth inning double but that he didn't want to embarrass the pitcher. When the subject turned to closer Mariano Rivera, the captain stated flatly that no one has ever done the things Mo has done and probably no one ever will again.

About thirty feet away, Jorge Posada was singing the praises of Pettitte, Rivera, and Jeter. Another six or seven lockers over, Mo was complimenting all his teammates, especially Jeter, Posada, and the winner, Pettitte, who must have been somewhere getting iced down. Except for the six-rows-deep crowd of Japanese reporters encircling Hideki Matsui, who in the eighth inning became the eighth Yankee in history to hit a pinch hit homerun in a World Series, the Jeter-Posada-Rivera media triangle was the center of the baseball universe.

It deserved to be. For approaching a generation now, Jeter, Posada, Rivera, and Pettitte have anchored baseball's most successful franchise. As it was in the clubhouse late Saturday night, only as many as three of them can be on the field at any one time. But except for Pettitte's three-year fling with the Houston Astros, the presence of all four veteran players is always felt on the field.

It was certainly felt in Game 3. Yes, relative newcomers like Alex Rodriguez, Matsui, and Nick Swisher hit the bombs, and Johnny Damon had the big two-RBI double during the fifth inning rally. But each of the ageless four owned a corner of the win.

The definition of a "quality start" is at least six innings and no more than three runs. Pettitte allowed four runs, all of them earned, in his six on the mound. But the Yankees got enough quality out of Pettitte to justify a contract extension. Two of the four runs came on Jayson Werth solo rockets, but that is almost a matter of course these days. Werth has been a monster, and not just on Halloween. Perhaps only Pettitte and Posada know why they served up the exact same curveball over the heart of the plate a second time to the Phillies rightfielder, but if you're going to gamble the time to do it is with the bases empty.

The highlight of Pettitte's outing—no tour de force by any stretch of the imagination—was the bottom of the second inning following Werth's first jack. The Phils began a whole new rally, which included a bunt single by Cole Hamels that found both Pettitte and A-Rod flatfooted. When Pettitte walked Jimmy Rollins on five pitches with the bases loaded, Phillies fans had visions of Chad Gaudin in long relief. But Pettitte and Posada, anchored mentally by a previous Yankees dynasty, were stoic without being stiff, getting Shane Victorino to fly out for a sacrifice and then freezing Chase Utley with a signature curve.

In the fifth inning, Andy Pettitte put on a brief hitting clinic by waiting on a Cole Hamels curveball that actually reached the plate a bit below the strike zone. Pettitte's gentle single to short left-centerfield did more than tie the score at 3-3. It upped the ante for Jeter and Damon, neither of whom wanted to be shown up by an American League pitcher.

Aside from handling five different Yankee pitchers intelligently and generally not letting the Phillies have their way on the bases, Posada had the grittiest at-bat of anyone in Game 3. In the seventh inning, Posada was turned around to bat lefty against right-handed reliever Chad Durbin. The Yankees catcher did not look stellar but battled to a full count before going with a pitch to left. The hooking single knocked in Damon, extended the New York lead to 7-4, and reminded 46,000 fans at Citizens Bank Park that old Yankees never die, they just kill you softly.

Jeter's night at the plate was nothing spectacular, but his fifth inning single just in front of the diving centerfielder Victorino kept a rally going. Perhaps more importantly, the captain handled everything in the field ably, including Jimmy Rollins's first inning swipe of second base. Rollins stole the bag mostly off of Pettitte, an impressive feat considering the Yankee lefty from the Bayou has been a pickoff machine for a decade and a half. But when Jeter and Rollins kidded afterwards at second base, Jeter playfully patted his Philadelphia counterpart on the helmet.

No one besides the two big game players knows exactly what was said, but the message to the rest of the world seemed to be: "Don't go anywhere. This game is just getting started." Not long after as the clock struck midnight and Rivera sawed off two bats to nail down a 2-1 Yankees Series lead, the same could be said for November baseball.

"Multilingual and multitalented: Jorge Posada."

JERRY COLEMAN ON THE YANKEES
AND PHILLIES 59 YEARS LATER

November 3, 2009

Former Yankees second baseman Jerry Coleman finished third in the balloting for American League Rookie of the Year in 1949. That same year he beat the Red Sox with a bases loaded triple in the ninth inning of the final regular season game to win the pennant for the Yanks

The following year, 1950, Coleman was the Most Valuable Player in the World Series between the Yankees and the Philadelphia Phillies. So for historic reasons alone, when the Yankees took care of business last Sunday night against the Angels, job number one was to track down Jerry Coleman.

Of course, when you're talking Jerry Coleman and history, the game of baseball and Coleman's on-the-field heroics during the Truman administration are only a small part of the picture.

Coleman was born in 1924 and raised in San Francisco during the Great Depression mostly by his mother. Things would have been just bearable on his father's $150-a-month salary from the U.S. Postal Service, but his dad turned mean when he drank. This led to a divorce, which left Jerry and his sister Rosemarie in a precarious position at a precarious time. The kids lived with their mom in a one-room flat on Fillmore Street and subsisted on $4.20 a week in government relief. One memory that has never quite left Jerry Coleman's consciousness was having to wear his sister's shoes to school when his only pair wore out.

One night Jerry's mom went out dancing to take her mind off the stress. What she didn't know was that as she danced, her ex-husband was lying in wait. He was convinced, erroneously, that there was another man in her life and took matters into his own hands. As she left the dance hall, her ex-husband shot her in the leg and the elbow.

Jerry's mom survived but spent nine months convalescing. Jerry and his sister were split up with relatives for a while, then eventually reunited with their mother, who now wore a permanent leg brace. In addition to regularly picking up a donated pot roast from a nearby soup kitchen, one of Jerry's many errands was to hike to the University of California Hospital for a replacement spring whenever his mother's brace broke down.

Coleman went on to serve as a fighter pilot with the United States Marines. In fact, he was the only Major League player to see combat in both World War II and the Korean War. In WWII, he flew dive bombing missions in the Solomon Islands and later in the Philippines. In the Korean War he flew a Corsair propeller plane and did more of the same. The war itself, however, was not the same.

While war, of course, changes a person, it seemed Coleman's second war changed him more than his first. In Korea he nearly lost his life twice, once in a near miss during another pilot's emergency runway landing, the second time in an errant takeoff that left Coleman trapped in a flipped over plane. But the worst experience by far was watching his best friend, Max Harper, getting blown out of the sky right in front of him.

When he returned from the Korean War, the Yankees held Jerry Coleman Day at the Stadium on September 13, 1953. The end of the war saw the division between North and South Korea at the 38th parallel right back where it started, leaving Coleman and many thousands of thoughtful fighting men ambivalent about the war's purpose. There were lingering demons to deal with, but not even Coleman could have guessed that the very same day he was reluctantly being dubbed a hero, his best friend's widow would show up unannounced. Coleman had the unenviable task of looking into Mrs. Harper's eyes and telling her that her husband really was gone.

During his young life, baseball was as much an escape for Jerry Coleman as anything else. In the 1950 World Series he turned in a peak performance at the right time. In Game 1, a 1-0 Yankees victory, he knocked in the only run with a sacrifice fly late in the game. In Game 2 he scored the Yankees only run in the first nine innings, allowing Joe DiMaggio to hit the game-winning homerun in the tenth. In Game 3 Coleman singled home Gene Woodling to give the Bombers a 3-2 walk-off win in the ninth. In those days, there was no pie in the face for Coleman or anyone else.

With all those qualifications, not to mention a Ford C. Frick Award for his decades of excellence broadcasting San Diego Padres games, who is better qualified to give an educated guess on this new Yankees-Phillies World Series? At first, Coleman called it about even, explaining that the power hitting is tremendous on both sides. The Phillies compiled their impressive numbers during the regular season without the help of a designated hitter, but on the negative side the Phils tend to strike out a lot.

Coleman gives the defensive edge to the Phillies. Central to that edge is the catching, spearheaded by Carlos Ruiz, who comes with a bonus. As someone who was brought in to handle the pitching and throw out runners, Ruiz has developed into a wildcard offensive threat at the bottom of the order.

But the key according to Coleman is the pitching, and the Yankees have the edge in the bullpen. Back in 1950, other than Robin Roberts the Phillies hurler who impressed Coleman the most was righty Jim Konstanty. Konstanty was National League Most Valuable Player that year as a reliever appearing in 74 games but started Game 1 of the World Series. He went on to stifle the Yanks in relief later in the Series, but the Yankees' pitching was a hair better overall. Loosely speaking, this year's Jim Konstanty could be named J.A. Happ or Pedro Martinez, but the Series will come down to relief, however that is defined.

Demonstrating that a Phillies-Yankees World Series is about as good as it gets no matter which century it's played in, Jerry Coleman called us an hour or so before Game 4 in support of Charlie Manuel's decision to go with Joe Blanton. Starting J.A. Happ in this situation, Coleman explained, could ruin a top prospect, and Cliff Lee's prowess was better left at full throttle for Game 5. No matter what happens, it's clear that the decorated pilot so instrumental in the last Yankees-Phillies postseason matchup is still on full throttle himself.

"Jerry and Billy."

The Long Steal

November 3, 2009

There was the Merkle Incident. There was the Called Shot. There was the Shot Heard Round the World. A handful of plays in the annals of baseball—some occurring in the postseason, some not—have risen not only to the heights of legend but to a rarified air where they are known universally by a given name free of context.

Johnny Damon's steal of second base then third base in one nearly continuous attempt during the ninth inning of Game 4 between the Yankees and Phillies may have attained that lofty position. The combination of its rarity, cold-blooded execution, and timeliness should qualify. The only thing the play is missing right now is a name.

Not just any name—a good one. One that you folks and we folks can reminisce and argue about in a mall or on a park bench sometime around the year 2040, when we can all claim to have been there yelling for Johnny to take off for third. We bandied about a few potential names early Monday morning in the bowels of Citizens Bank Park.

The One-Man Double-Steal seemed cumbersome. The First-to-Third Steal seemed unspectacular. Around 3:15 AM we settled on the Long Steal. It's pithy, a bit mysterious sounding, and suggestive of American sports mythology in the vein of the Long Count. You and your equally sleep-deprived friends may come up with a better name, and if you do we expect to hear about it. But for now, the Long Steal is all we've got.

Any great play needs some sort of a worthy setup, and the Long Steal was no exception. The over-shift on Mark Texeira has a history all its own. Fans of baseball in the new millennium may identify it with Jason Giambi among other lefty pull-hitters, but the over-shift goes back at least as far as the greatest pure hitter of all time, Ted Williams. There were multiple variations depending on where the shortstop and third baseman were willing to relocate, but the idea was the same: Here is a dead-pull hitter either unable to go the opposite way, too proud, or some combination of the two. Ted was simply too proud. He could have hit about .800 against the shift and without bunting.

The second precondition for the Long Steal was reliever Brad Lidge's unwillingness to hold runners on. This is not a rub. Lidge knows where his bread is buttered and has reached heights other closers only dream of. But the Yankees under manager Joe Girardi—like the Phillies under Charlie Manuel—will exploit any weakness, more so now than ever.

Which brings us to the third precondition. Johnny Damon has fifteen years experience in the big leagues. He is a smart, alert player who has continued to grow as an athlete even on the downhill side of his speed afoot. The Long Steal actually started during Damon's at-bat just prior. No matter what the hosts of local late night radio call-in sports shows scream, Lidge had his stuff Sunday night. The fastball was fast, the slider moving sharply yet unpredictably, and Lidge himself had a swagger reminiscent of last October.

When the count hit 1-2, it was the Yankees who had their backs against the wall. Lidge had made quick work of Hideki Matsui on a pop out and then dominated Derek Jeter, who waved at a slider for strike three. Damon quickly occupied that same hole, and baseball brains all around the park had it mapped out like a drone sent into the hills of Afghanistan: Damon fans; Stairs, Rollins, Victorino, or Utley goes yard against Rivera; Lee tears it up in Game 5; and the series returns to Yankee Stadium with the Bombers on the precipice of elimination.

But something funny happened on the way to the Bronx. Johnny Damon worked a World Series at-bat that would have made Wade Boggs proud. He fouled off pitch after pitch, each time letting just a little air out of the Philadelphia balloon until finally he saw something he could get most of the barrel on.

Damon is capable of such things. Five years ago he hit a grand salami for the Red Sox in the final game of the AL Championship Series to put the last nail in the Yankees' coffin. Not a power hitter, Damon developed a quick inside swing to take advantage of short right field porches. He has a killer instinct, and he killed the Yankees. That's why the Yankees went out and got him.

Great plays sometimes need not only preconditions but post-conditions. The Long Steal was one such play. Had Alex Rodriguez left Damon stranded at third, the Long Steal would have become merely a footnote or a trivia question by Wednesday. But this play had the requisite dramatic ending, and so it is granted eternal baseball life. Write it down on your calendar. When we're all much older and not much wiser, we have a date to watch grainy highlight films together. Even if they're not grainy.

"How to stay loose."

BASEBALL PARADISE

November 4, 2009

The Yankees and Phillies are both ready for tonight, and so are we. With the entire 2009 season coming down to a game or two in the Bronx, preparation is key, especially for fans ducking verbal heaters thrown high and tight by their Turnpike counterparts.

If you're a Yankee fan, of course, you can brag that you only have to win one, and it will be where your team has the best home field record in all of baseball. Andy Pettitte has already won four World Series games in his illustrious career and 17 altogether in postseason play. His lefty delivery was made for the Stadium, or perhaps the Stadium was made for it. C.C. Sabathia is waiting in the wings for a Game 7 if necessary, and you've already seen how effective he is on three days' rest.

You Phanatic phools can gloat all you want about knocking out A.J. Burnett in the third inning, but the fact is the outing was a fluke and having thrown only 53 pitches Monday night, he's available for long relief in the unlikely event that becomes necessary. Cliff Lee, on the other hand, threw 112 pitches in a less-than-stellar performance and is done for the series other than as a Code Red emergency reliever. We'll take our chances.

The truth is, you Philly phreaks, our team has dominated your team with Mark Teixeira hitting a little over a buck. What happens when his bat shows up? In the meantime, how many more times can you plunk A-Rod before sending your starting pitcher—that is, whomever you select by lottery—to the showers for the winter? A-Rod has your number, and so do the umpires. You're going to have to pitch to Alex, and please, enough with the choke talk. Rodriguez got over his postseason jitters a month ago, and you know it. So does Brad Lidge. And did we mention that Mariano Rivera is the greatest postseason closer of all time and is incredibly well rested? Or that you can't steal signs in our house?

If you're a Phillies fan, you don't have to take it. Naturally, you can shout from the rafters that your team is still the reigning World Champion and has yet to be knocked from that perch. The Phillies may have struggled at home at times during the season, but guess where they made up for it?

And please, send Andy Pettitte back to the '90s, where he belongs. Pedro Martinez is a World Series Champion in *this* decade and has the Yankees dialed in. No one could be less intimidated by the Bombers and their over-inflated mystique. Ask Don Zimmer. When it comes time for Game 7, we'll take that Lee-Burnett all-Arkansas reprise in the sixth, seventh, or whenever you want it. Unless you'd like to serve us Phil Coke again. Phillies go better with Coke.

Send Tex back to Texas. When the real Ryan Howard shows up, which will be any minute now, you'll finally understand why his first four full seasons have caused Ruthian comparisons, and right in the house that A-Rod built. Chase Utley owns the Yankees pitching staff. He's already passed the Babe and that Gehrig dude and will surpass Reggie Jackson's World Series record without hot-dogging it at home plate. So as you get scalped, enjoy the three thousand dollars you paid a scalper. The Phillies will see to it that you get your money's Werth.

Okay, everyone, listen up. Before we continue hurling cheesesteaks and Yankee Franks, we need to stop for a moment and remember how lucky we really are. At least if you live within a hundred-mile radius of Trenton, no one could have scripted the 2009 season better than a final showdown in the Bronx between the National League's best team and the American League's best team separated by an hour-and-a-half Amtrak ride.

While we're busy searching the crowd for navy blue or bright red pinstripes to pour beer on, let us recall that in this inaugural season at the new Yankee Stadium, history will look back kindly on this match-up of titans. The Yankees have three sure Hall of Famers—Jeter, Rivera, and Rodriguez—and possibly as many as four more one day—Pettitte,

Posada, Sabathia, and Teixeira. The Phillies have first-ballot inductee Pedro Martinez and enough Hall prospects to fill an aisle of their own—Howard, Utley, Rollins, and Lee. As the Reverend Jesse Jackson might say, "If they are great, don't hate."

Looking more to the here and now, the two teams have played largely errorless baseball and have both lived up to their reputations of never quitting. They are gutsy players who leave their big contracts with their accountants and on the field serve as role models for Little Leaguers everywhere. Even if global warming continues to cooperate, November baseball may not see the likes of two so evenly matched and fiercely competitive teams for a long, long time to come.

Now resume chanting obscenities. And play ball!

"The NL's answer to Reggie Jackson."

WINTERBALL, ANYONE?

November 6, 2009

Game 6 of the World Series didn't turn out to be the nail-biter we might have expected, but there were so many nail-biting moments throughout the series it hardly mattered. As much as the Phillies were said to have an American League lineup, it fell short in the American League park, where the Yankees inserted a real DH into their own lineup. Hideki Matsui, a terrific hitter to begin with, settled into that role fulltime this season, and his comfort level paid off for the Yankees with their twenty-seventh championship.

Chances are at least one of these two great teams will be back next fall, maybe both. Ruben Amaro will be looking to acquire more offensive punch off the bench, (Thome, Delgado, Giambi) and not just for the Phillies' probable return to the World Series. And although there aren't too many Cliff Lees out there, there is Cliff Lee himself. The Phils have already picked up his option for 2010, and the front office is looking hard for a sure-thing number two starter. Meanwhile, even if J.C. Romero is a hundred percent by March, there is no one on the planet who believes the bullpen will remain intact.

But the core of the Phillies—Utley, Rollins, Howard, Werth, Victorino, and Ruiz—are in their prime, and Feliz and Ibanez look like there's still some gas in the tank. This lineup ain't broke, even if the Yankee lefties had their number for a couple of games. Unless body language and win-loss records lie, to a man they love playing for Charlie Manuel. This isn't 1981 with George Steinbrenner at the helm.

Disemboweling a team that fell two steps short of the mountaintop is out of the question when the mountaintop will remain within reach for at least a few more years.

As for the real Steinbrenner, or the front office team he's left in place, there will be tinkering under the hood in spite of the champagne, but no rebuilt engine. Jeter has a long way to go to 4,000 hits. Rivera will close until he no longer can. Pettitte's not quite ready to walk away a la Mike Mussina. Francisco Cervelli is the heir apparent to Jorge Posada, but Georgie can still hit a ton. The right sight of the infield and outfield is youthful and locked up. Re-signing Damon and Matsui are the big offensive conundrums, but both made solid arguments in the postseason for another year or two. Austin Jackson will be brought further up the ladder, but all the youth in the world can't replace that kind of clutch.

With the return of Chien-Ming Wang unknown, Brian Cashman is already gearing up to sign a fourth starter, or what teams with less money call a number one starter. Hungover though they may be, Yankee fans know in their hearts they were one Matsui away from a Game 7. In that Game 7, a tired Sabathia left arm would have left Girardi scrambling for five innings of middle relief without the cushion of a tomorrow. The fact is, while Girardi's three-man World Series rotation was a stroke of genius, it was also a stroke of luck. The Steinbrenner gang will not face next fall without a fourth wheel.

Beyond the two best teams in the game, the national pastime itself is looking surprisingly good right now. Attendance is high even with some steep ticket pricing during a recession. There is more grass and less Astroturf. The World Series has never been truly global, but with much of Latin America represented and parts of Asia too, it's certainly getting closer. It may be merely anecdotal, but we see more kids running out to nearby fields to hit fungoes than just five or ten years ago. And stars like Jimmy Rollins and Torii Hunter are doing their part and more to get African-American kids interested in the game.

Even the steroid era seems to be fading from the American consciousness. The Selena Roberts hatchet job book on A-Rod sold just a handful of copies because in this otherwise imperfect society, confessions have the ability to purify and insulate. Moreover, when the two American League homerun leaders are tied at 39, you know the steroid problem is largely in the rear view mirror.

There is, however, one thing the game should fear, even more than fear itself—December baseball. It's not that farfetched. From where we are today, what would it really take? A few more rainouts. A couple more TV days off during the Divisional and Championship Series. A strike. God forbid another attack on our nation. A couple of snowouts. A few more expansion teams and another wild card round.

Pretty soon you're eating turkey and flipping back and forth between the Cowboys-Lions game and the Fall (Winter?) Classic. Pretty soon MLB.com is selling Under Armour with the Florida Marlins logo on it. Pretty soon you've got bowl games and neutral sites in the Deep South and the Sun Belt, where cheerleaders and pom-pons cause interference as Dustin Pedroia chases down a ball in foul territory.

"Why not just build a whole bunch of domed stadiums?" some ask. The answer is we've already got a cold weather league that plays indoors during ever-elongating postseasons as fan interest gradually dwindles. It's called the NHL.

Godzilla waiting to destroy.

A Swish and a smile."

ABOUT THE AUTHORS

Billy Staples

After a childhood spent on sandlots and in Major League clubhouses, in 1993 Billy Staples graduated Phi Beta Kappa from East Stroudsburg University and became an inner city English teacher in Bethlehem, Pennsylvania. Over the next 13 years he used his friendships with ballplayers and their willingness to sign autographs as a motivational technique to get his students to come to school, behave, and do their work. Billy told each student, "I don't teach Monday through Friday or September through June. I'll teach you nights, weekends, summers and the rest of your life if you are willing to learn."

Billy was twice nominated for Disney's National Teacher of the Year award. His groundbreaking work helping troubled kids fix their lives and make it to college was featured in a five-part series on CNN. Staples sits on the board of BEST, a college scholarship organization he helped start under the guidance of Linny Fowler and Jack Canfield, author of the *Chicken Soup for the Soul* book series. BEST has helped over forty at-risk, financially challenged students from the Lehigh Valley, PA/ Phillipsburg, NJ area to attend and pay for college. Staples's friendship with Jack Canfield has also helped what was once just an idea for a motivational book series to come to fruition as *Before the Glory*, the book he and Rich Herschlag completed in 2007. In the foreword to the book Canfield wrote, "Billy is a living example of *The Success Principles* and *The Secret*," both of which have sold millions of copies.

Since then, Billy has toured the U.S. and several Latin American countries to spread his positive message. He and Rich Herschlag have, meanwhile, extended their range by co-writing an inspirational baseball column. Somewhere in the middle of it all, Billy completed his master's degree in education and administration at East Stroudsburg University.

Billy Staples can be reached for personal appearances at www. billystaples.com or on Facebook.

"Billy with number 1, Bobby Murcer."

Rich Herschlag

Rich Herschlag's published books include *Jack of All Trades* (Northwest, 1994*), Lay Low and Don't Make the Big Mistak*e (Simon & Schuster, 1997), *The Interceptor* (Ballantine, 1998), *Women Are From Manhattan, Men Are From Brooklyn* (Black Maverick, 2002), and *Before the Glory* (HCI, 2007).

Lay Low, a humorous but practical guide to gliding through corporate America on minimal effort, resulted in over 175 radio and TV interviews across the country. The book was the subject of a feature article in *USA Today*, highlighted in *Reader's Digest*, and quoted on the front page of the *Wall Street Journal. Lay Low* was also translated into Chinese.

The Interceptor, a political and environmental thriller set above and below the streets of New York, was reviewed favorably by numerous publications including the *New York Times*, the *New York Daily News*, and the *New York Post.*

Herschlag's forthcoming book, *Sinatra, Gotti and Me*, co-written with Tony Delvecchio, is a firsthand account of Delvecchio's tumultuous years running Jilly's, the legendary New York nightclub.

Rich Herschlag earned a bachelor's degree in science and engineering from Princeton University in 1984. In 1991 he received his license as a professional engineer from the State of New York and went to work as Chief Borough Engineer for the Office of the Manhattan Borough President, where he stayed until early 1995. Since then he has run a consulting business, Turnkey Structural, that specializes in the rehabilitation of older residential and commercial buildings. The website is www.turnkeystructural.com

Herschlag lives in Easton, PA, with Susan, his wife of twenty-two years, and their daughters Rachel, 17, and Elise, 12.

"Rich relaxing in his living room."

Breinigsville, PA USA
17 October 2010
247466BV00006B/2/P